Accounts
Demystified

Books to make you better

Books to make you better. To make you *be* better, *do* better, *feel* better. Whether you want to upgrade your personal skills or change your job, whether you want to improve your managerial style, become a more powerful communicator, or be stimulated and inspired as you work.

Prentice Hall Business is leading the field with a new breed of skills, careers and development books. Books that are a cut above the mainstream – in topic, content and delivery – with an edge and verve that will make you better, with less effort.

Books that are as sharp and smart as you are.

Prentice Hall Business.
We work harder – so you don't have to.

For more details on products, and to contact us, visit
www.business-minds.com
www.yourmomentum.com

ANTHONY RICE

Accounts Demystified

How to understand financial accounting and analysis

Prentice Hall BUSINESS

an imprint of Pearson Education

London • New York • Toronto • Sydney • Tokyo • Singapore • Hong Kong • Cape Town
New Delhi • Madrid • Paris • Amsterdam • Munich • Milan • Stockholm

PEARSON EDUCATION LIMITED

Edinburgh Gate
Harlow CM20 2JE
Tel: +44 (0)1279 623623
Fax: +44 (0)1279 431059

Website: www.pearsoned.co.uk

ISBN 0 273 66334 8

British Library Cataloguing in Publication Data
A CIP catalogue record for this book can be obtained from the British Library

10 9 8 7 6 5 4

Typeset by Northern Phototypesetting Co. Ltd, Bolton
Printed and bound in Great Britain by Bell & Bain Ltd, Glasgow

The Publishers' policy is to use paper manufactured from sustainable forests.

Contents

Part I: The basics of accounting

Preface

A glance at the accounts of most of Britain's larger companies could lead you to conclude that accounting is a very complex and technical subject.

While it can be both of these things, accounting is actually based on an incredibly simple principle which was devised more than 500 years ago and has remained unchanged ever since. The apparent complexity of many companies' accounts results from the rules and terminology that have developed around this fundamental principle to accommodate modern business practices.

I believe that, once you really understand the fundamental principle and how it is applied, you will find that the rules and terminology follow logically and easily. This view determines the arrangement of the chapters in *Accounts Demystified* and it is important, therefore, to read them chronologically. You may, however, omit Chapter Five, which discusses book-keeping jargon and Chapter Seven, which concentrates on more sophisticated areas of accounting, without losing the thread of the book.

May I also suggest that, before you reach Chapter Six, you photocopy the key parts of Wingate Foods' accounts (pages 278 to 285). From Chapter Six onwards, the text refers to these pages frequently and you will find it much easier with copies in front of you.

If you have any comments on the book, you are welcome to email me at ar@demystifyme.com

Anthony Rice

This book is dedicated
to Charlotte

Acknowledgements

A number of people have contributed to this book.

I am especially grateful to Jonathan Munday and Simon Rees, partners of accountants Rees Pollock. Jonathan reviewed this edition in detail and helped update the book for the large number of new rules that have been instituted since first publication. In some cases, I have decided to live with technical errors and omissions in the interests of clarity. For such decisions I am solely responsible.

I would also like to thank the following who volunteered to read this book and all of whom made valuable comments and suggestions: Michael Gaston, Debbie Hastings-Henry, Steve Holt, Alex Johnstone, Keith Murray, Jamie Reeve, Brian Rice, Clive Richardson, David Tredrea, Martin Whittle, Charlie Wrench.

Anthony Rice

Prologue

Sarah

Sarah is the owner and sole employee of a company called Silk Bloomers Limited (known as SBL). Just over a year ago, she went on a business trip to the Far East where, by chance, she came across a company producing silk plants and flowers of exceptional quality. On her return to the UK she immediately quit her job and set up SBL (with £10,000 of her own money) to import and distribute these silk plants.

Sarah is a born entrepreneur and the prospects for her business look extremely good. Her only problem is that, since the company has just finished its first year, she has to produce the annual accounts. She has kept good records of all the transactions the company made during the year, but she doesn't know how to translate them into the required financial statements. She is determined not to pay her accountants a big fee to do it for her.

Tom

Tom has two problems.

The first relates to his employer, Wingate Foods, where he is sales manager. Wingate manufactures confectionery and chocolate biscuits, mostly for the big supermarkets to sell under their own names. Four years ago, the company appointed a new managing director who immediately embarked on an aggressive expansion programme.

Tom's concern is that the managing director seems to want to win orders at almost any cost. Simultaneously, the company is spending a lot of money on new offices and machinery. The managing director is

brimming with confidence and continually refers to the steady rise in sales, profits and dividends. Nonetheless, Tom has the nagging suspicion that something is badly wrong. He just can't put his finger on it.

Tom's other 'problem' is that he has some spare cash which is currently on deposit at the bank. Tom doesn't have Sarah's entrepreneurial spirit and there's no chance of him risking his money on starting a business. He feels, though, that he should perhaps risk a small amount on the stock market. He has been given a couple of 'tips' but would like to check them out for himself.

Tom has therefore decided it is time to learn how to read company accounts so he can form his own opinion of both Wingate and his prospective investments.

Chris

Chris is a financial journalist for a national newspaper who, although not an accountant, can read and analyse company accounts with confidence.

This was not always the case. Chris used to be one of the thousands of people who understand a profit and loss account but find the balance sheet a total mystery. A few years ago, however, a friend explained the fundamental principle of accounting to him and showed him how everything else follows logically from it. Within hours, his understanding of balance sheets and everything else to do with company accounts was transformed.

Recently, Tom and Sarah mentioned their respective accounting problems to Chris. Chris began enthusing about the approach he had been taught and how easy it all was once you really understood the basics. Sarah, never one to miss an opportunity, immediately demanded that Chris should give up his weekend to share the 'secret' with Tom and herself.

Introduction

Wingate's annual report

Before we do anything, I think we should have a quick look at Wingate's most recent **annual report and accounts** (which is what we really mean by the phrase 'annual report'). We are going to be referring to this a lot and I think you'll find it helpful to get to know your way around it now. It will also give you an idea of what we're trying to achieve. By the end of this weekend, you should not only understand everything in this annual report, you should also be able to analyse it in detail.

The other thing I should do is give you a brief outline of how I plan to structure the weekend in order to achieve that objective. After that, we might as well go straight into the first session.

Wingate's annual report for year five [reproduced on pages 275 to 285] is a fairly typical annual report for a medium-sized company. As you can see, it consists of six items:

- **Directors' report**
- **Auditors' report**
- **Profit & loss account**
- **Balance sheet**
- **Cash flow statement**
- **Notes to the accounts**

The **directors' report** and the **auditors' report** don't usually tell us a great deal. You must always read them, however, particularly the auditors' report. We'll come back to them later and see why.

The **profit & loss account** (the 'P&L', for short), the **balance sheet** and the **cash flow statement** are the real heart of an annual report. Everything we're going to talk about is really geared towards helping you to understand and analyse these three 'statements'.

The **notes to the accounts** are a lot more than just footnotes. They contain many extremely valuable details which supplement the information in the three main statements. You can't do any meaningful analysis of a company without them.

You do realise, Chris, that I hardly understand a word of what I'm looking at here?

Structure outline

That's fine. I'm going to assume you know absolutely nothing and take it very slowly. What we're going to do is to break the weekend up into 12 separate sessions which fall into three distinct parts:

I   The basics of accounting

II   Interpretation of accounts

III Analysing company accounts

I The basics of accounting

The basics will take up our first four sessions.

- In the **first session**, I will explain what a balance sheet is and how it relates to the fundamental principle of accounting.

- **Session 2** will be spent actually drawing up the balance sheet for your company, Sarah. I know you're not interested in creating accounts, Tom, but this session is important to understanding how the fundamental principle is applied in practice.

- In session 3, I will explain, briefly as it's very straightforward, what a P&L and cash flow statement are and how they are related to the balance sheet.

- Then in **session 4**, we will actually draw up the P&L and cash flow statement for SBL.

- Finally, in **session 5**, I will introduce you to some jargon you may actually find useful.

Why are you starting with the balance sheet? In Wingate's annual report, the P&L comes first and that's the bit I vaguely understand. Shouldn't we start there?

No, we should not. The balance sheet really ought to come before the P&L; you'll see why later.

II Interpretation of accounts

At the end of **session 5**, you should understand the basics of accounting and you may well find that you can look at Wingate's accounts and understand the vast majority of what's in there!

There are, however, quite a few rules and a lot of terminology that we need to cover before you can read any set of company accounts with confidence.

- In **session 6**, we will work our way through the whole of Wingate's accounts, which will bring out most of the features you are likely to encounter in the average company.

- In **session 7**, I will briefly explain some further features of accounts which are common in larger companies; these, after all, are the companies you are likely to be investing in, Tom.

III Analysing company accounts

It's all very well to know what a company's accounts mean, but it doesn't actually give you any insight into the company. That's why you have to know how to analyse accounts.

I will start, in **session 8**, by introducing the whole subject of financial analysis to make sure we are all clear about what companies are trying to achieve and how, for the purposes of analysis, we separate a company into two components – the enterprise and the funding structure.

In **sessions 9 and 10** respectively we will then analyse the enterprise and the funding structure of Wingate Foods.

Up to this point, all our analysis will have been about understanding the financial performance of companies. We will not have related any of it to the value of the company, which is what potential investors are interested in. I do not plan to go into detailed investment analysis but I will, in **session 11**, explain how most investors relate the performance of a company to its valuation.

I will end, in **session 12**, with a summary of how, through a combination of careful presentation and creative accounting, companies try to 'sell' themselves to investors.

After that, you're on your own.

The basics of accounting

As well as listing your assets and liabilities and showing that you are worth £31,000, your balance sheet also shows *how* you came to be worth that much.

CHAPTER 1

The balance sheet and the fundamental principle

- Assets, liabilities and balance sheets
- Sarah's 'personal' balance sheet
- The balance sheet of a company
- The balance sheet chart
- Summary

What I'm going to do first is explain what assets and liabilities are, which may seem trivial but it's important there are no misunderstandings. Next, I will explain what a balance sheet is and show you how to draw up your own personal balance sheet. We will then relate this to a company's balance sheet.

At that point, I will, finally, explain what I mean by the fundamental principle of accounting and you will see that the balance sheet is just the principle put into practice. I will also show you how we can represent the balance sheet in chart form, which I think you will find a lot easier to handle than tables full of numbers.

Then we'll take a break before we actually set about building up SBL's balance sheet.

Assets, liabilities and balance sheets

Typically, individuals and companies both have assets and liabilities.

An **asset** can be one of two things. It is either:

- something you own; for example, money, land, buildings, goods, brand names, shares in other companies etc., or

- something you are owed by someone else, i.e. something which is technically yours, but is currently in someone else's possession. More often than not, it's money you are owed, but it could be anything.

A **liability** is anything you owe to someone else and expect to have to hand over in due course. Liabilities are usually money, but they can be anything.

A **balance sheet** is just a table, listing all someone's assets and liabilities, along with the value of each of those assets and liabilities at a particular point in time.

Sarah's 'personal' balance sheet

You can't say that's a difficult concept, can you? Let's see how it works by writing down on a single sheet of paper all Sarah's assets and liabilities. We will then have effectively drawn up her **personal balance sheet**. I think you'll find it pretty interesting [See Table 1.1.]

The top part of this is fine, Chris. We've just got a simple list of all my main assets and their values. We've also got a list of the amounts that I owe to other people.

There are several things here, though, that I don't understand. Why are the liabilities in brackets and what do you mean by 'Net assets' – I'm never sure what people are talking about when they use the word 'net'.

'Net' just means the value of something after having deducted something else. The reason you're never sure what people mean is that they don't explain what it is they're deducting.

SARAH'S PERSONAL BALANCE SHEET
As at today

	£	£
Assets		
House/contents	50,000	
Investment in SBL	10,000	
Pension scheme	2,000	
Jewellery	1,000	
Loan to brother	500	
Total		63,500
Liabilities		
Mortgage	(30,000)	
Credit card	(500)	
Overdraft at bank	(1,500)	
Phone bill outstanding	(500)	
Total		(32,500)
Net assets		31,000
Net worth		
Inheritance	20,000	
Savings	11,000	
Total		31,000

Note: Brackets are used to signify negative numbers.

Table 1.1 Sarah's personal balance sheet

In this case, we add up all your assets, which total £63,500. These are your **gross assets**, although we usually leave out the 'gross' and just call them your 'assets'. We then deduct all your liabilities from these assets. The brackets are common notation in the accounting world to

indicate negative numbers, because minus signs can be mistaken for dashes. Your liabilities total £32,500 so when we deduct this figure from your gross assets we are left with £31,000. These are your **net assets**.

Your net assets are what you would have left if you sold all your assets for the amounts shown and paid off all your liabilities. In other words, your net assets are what you are worth.

OK, so we've listed my assets and liabilities and shown what the net value of them is. That seems to fit your description of a balance sheet. So what's this whole bit at the bottom headed 'Net worth'?

A fair question. My description of a balance sheet wasn't entirely accurate. As well as listing your assets and liabilities and showing that you are worth £31,000, your balance sheet also shows how you came to be worth that much.

So how could you have come to be worth £31,000? There are only two ways:

1 You could have been given some of your assets. In your case you inherited £20,000. This is effectively what you 'started' out in life with; you didn't have to earn it.

2 You could have saved some of your earnings since you first started work. I don't just mean savings in the form of cash in a bank account or under your bed. I also include savings in the form of any asset that you could sell and turn into cash, such as your house, jewellery etc. In other words, your savings means all your earnings that you haven't spent on things like food, drink and holidays, which are gone for ever.

In your case, you have saved a total of £11,000 in your life so far. To emphasise the point, notice that your balance sheet does not show £11,000 in cash; your £11,000 savings are in the form of various assets.

Naturally, what you have been given plus what you have saved must be what you are worth today, i.e. it must equal your net assets. This is what we call the **balance sheet equation**:

> **Net worth = Assets – Liabilities**
> **(gross)**

Fine. That all seems pretty simple. What's it got to do with company accounts?

Everything. A company's balance sheet is exactly the same thing.

The balance sheet of a company

Let me just summarise Wingate's balance sheet for you and you'll see what I mean. A company can have all sorts of assets and liabilities which I'll come on to later (if you're still with me). For the moment, I'll group them into a few simple categories [see Table 1.2].

We're going to come across these categories a lot so you ought to know right away what they are:

- **Fixed assets** are any assets which a company uses on a long-term continuing basis (as opposed to assets which are bought to be sold on to customers); e.g. buildings, machinery, vehicles, computers.
- **Current assets** are assets you expect to sell or turn into cash within one year; e.g. stocks, amounts owed to you by customers.
- **Current liabilities** are liabilities that you expect to pay within the next year; e.g. amounts owed to suppliers.
- **Long-term liabilities** are liabilities you expect to have to pay, but not within the next year; e.g. loans from banks.

WINGATE FOODS PLC

Balance sheet at 31 December, year five

		£'000
Assets		
Fixed assets	5,326	
Current assets	2,817	
Total assets		8,143
Liabilities		
Current liabilities	(2,372)	
Long-term liabilities	(3,000)	
Total liabilities		(5,372)
Net assets		2,771
Shareholders' equity		
Capital invested	325	
Retained profit	2,446	
Total shareholders' equity		2,771

Table 1.2 Wingate's summary balance sheet

Just as we did for your personal balance sheet, Sarah, we can add up all the assets and deduct all the liabilities to get the company's net assets:

$$£8,143k - £5,372k = £2,771k$$

I use the letter 'k' to represent thousands, just as we use the letter 'm' to represent millions. So £8,143k is equivalent to £8,143,000 or £8.143m. It's a convenient shorthand, which I will use from now on.

Now look at the section labelled **shareholders' equity**. This is exactly the same as the section on your personal balance sheet labelled 'net worth' – it's just another phrase for it. As with your personal balance sheet, it shows how the net assets of the company were arrived at.

Capital invested is the amount of money put into the company by the shareholders (i.e. the owners). In other words, it is what the company 'starts with'. It is the equivalent of 'inheritance' on your personal balance sheet.

Although I say it's what the company 'starts with', I don't mean just money invested when the company first starts up. I include money invested by the shareholders at any time, in the same way as you might get an inheritance at any point in your life. The point is that it is money the company has not had to earn.

Retained profit is what the company has earned or 'saved'. A company sells products or services for which the customers pay. The company, of course, has to pay various expenses (to buy materials, pay staff, etc.).

Hopefully, what the company earns from its customers is more than the expenses and thus the company has made a profit.

The company then pays out *some* of these profits to the taxman and to the shareholders. What is left over is known as retained profit. This is equivalent to the 'savings' on your personal balance sheet.

When we said you had savings of £11,000, Sarah, I emphasised that this did not mean that you had £11,000 sitting in a bank account somewhere. Similarly, retained profit is very rarely all money; usually it is made up of all sorts of different assets.

So presumably your balance sheet equation applies in just the same way?

Yes, it looks like this:

> **Shareholders' equity**   **=**   **Assets – Liabilities**
> 2,771   =   8,143 – 5,372

The balance sheet equation rearranged

So, if I understand you correctly, Chris, the net assets are what would be left over if all the assets were sold and the liabilities paid off. This amount would belong to the shareholders; hence the term 'shareholders' equity' which is just another phrase, really, for the net assets. Is that right?

Yes.

*So the company doesn't **ultimately** own anything. I mean, it's got all these assets, but if it sold them it would have to pay off its liabilities and then give the rest of the proceeds to the shareholders.*

Yes, that's right. After all, a company is just a legal framework for a group of investors (i.e. the shareholders) to organise their investment. Ultimately, *people* own things, not companies. This way of looking at a company's balance sheet leads us to write the balance sheet equation slightly differently:

> **Assets**   **=**   **Shareholders' equity + Liabilities**
> 8,143   =   2,771   +   5,372

This is what your maths teacher at school used to call 'rearranging the equation'. What it's saying is that the assets must add up exactly to the liabilities plus the shareholders' equity.

We can simplify the balance sheet equation even more if we want. As you just said, all the company's assets are effectively owed to someone, whether it be employees, suppliers, banks or shareholders. *Someone* has a claim over each and every one of the assets. Thus we can say that the assets must equal the **claims** on the assets:

$$\textbf{Assets} = \textbf{Claims}$$

This equation is the **fundamental principle of accounting**: at all times the assets of a company must equal the claims over those assets. As you can see, the balance sheet is just the principle put into practice. By the time we have finished, you will see how everything to do with company accounts hinges on this principle.

One of the benefits of looking at a balance sheet in this simple way is that we can display it as a chart, which will make it a lot easier to see what's going on when we start building up SBL's balance sheet.

The balance sheet chart

The **balance sheet chart** [Figure 1.1] consists of two **bars**, each of which consists of a number of **boxes**. These should be interpreted as follows:

- The height of each box is the value of the relevant asset or liability.
- The **assets bar** (the left-hand bar) has all the assets of the company

stacked on top of one another. The height of the bar thus shows the total (i.e. gross) value of all the assets of the company.

If you compare this chart with Wingate's summary balance sheet [page 8 – Table 1.2] you will see that we have a fixed assets box with a height of £5,326k and a current assets box with a height of £2,817k. The height of the bar is £8,143k, which is the total value of all Wingate's assets.

- The **claims bar** (the right-hand bar) shows all the claims over the assets of the company. At the top we show the liabilities to third parties which the company must pay at some point. At the bottom we show the claims of the shareholders (the shareholders' equity) which the shareholders would get if all the assets were sold off.

Again, we can compare this bar to Wingate's summary balance sheet [page 8] and see how the heights of the boxes match the individual

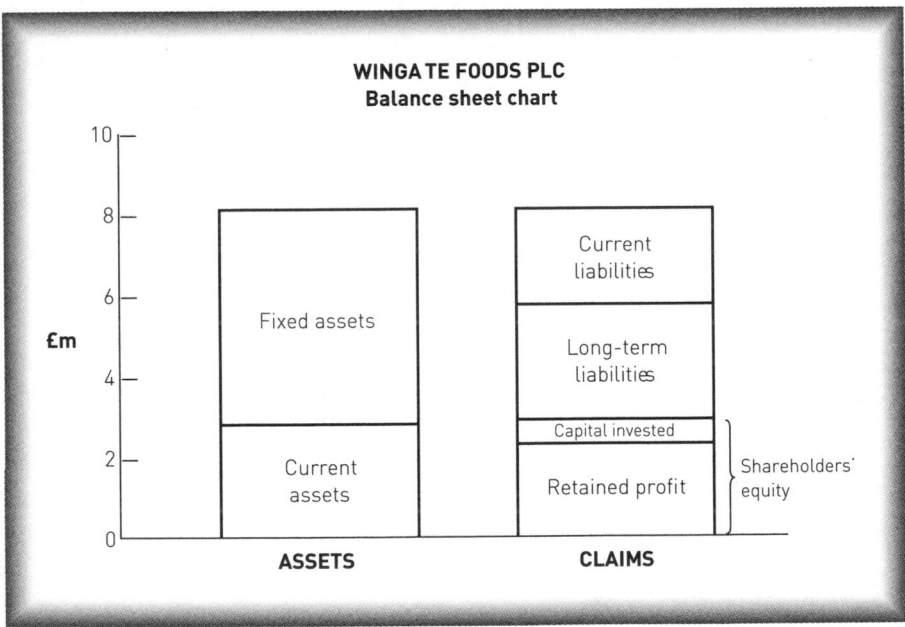

Figure 1.1 Wingate's balance sheet chart

items. As you would expect, the height of the bar is the sum of the liabilities and the shareholders' equity.

The most important thing about this diagram is that the two bars are the same height. This must be true by definition of our balance sheet equation.

When a company is in business (i.e. 'trading') all the different items that make up its balance sheet will be continually changing. On our balance sheet chart this means that both the heights of the bars and the heights of the boxes will change. Whatever happens, though, the height of the assets bar will always be the same as the height of the claims bar.

As you explain it here, Chris, I think I get it. In fact, it all looks fairly straightforward. I'm pretty sure, though, that I couldn't go away and draw up SBL's balance sheet on my own.

Maybe not, but in a couple of hours' time you will be able to, I promise. You'll be amazed how easy it is. Before we get on to that, though, let's just summarise what we've covered so far.

SUMMARY

- An asset is something a company either owns or is owed by someone else.

- A liability is something a company owes to someone else.

- A company's balance sheet consists of two things:

  1 A list of the company's assets and liabilities, their value at a particular moment in time and therefore what the company's net assets are; this is the value 'due' to the shareholders.

  2 An explanation of how the net assets came to be what they are. There are only two ways:
     (a) The shareholders invested money in the company.
     (b) The company made a profit, a proportion of which it retained (rather than paying it out to the shareholders).

- Someone, either a third party or the shareholders, has a claim over each and every asset of the company.

- Thus, whatever happens, the assets must always equal the claims over the assets. This is the fundamental principle of accounting.

We create a balance sheet at a particular date by entering all the transactions the company makes up to that date and then making various adjustments.

Creating a balance sheet

- Procedure for creating a balance sheet
- SBL's balance sheet
- The different forms of balance sheet
- Basic concepts of accounting
- Summary

Now you know what a balance sheet is and how to look at one as a chart, we're ready to set about actually creating one. First, I'll briefly describe the procedure and then we'll build up SBL's balance sheet step by step.

Procedure for creating a balance sheet

We create a balance sheet at a particular date by entering all the **transactions** the company makes up to that date and then making various **adjustments**:

- A **transaction** is anything that the company does which affects its financial position. This includes raising money from shareholders and banks, buying materials, paying staff, selling products, etc.

  Naturally, large companies make many thousands of transactions each year which is why they have computers and large accounts departments. The accounting principle, however, is exactly the same, whatever the size of the company.

- As you will see, even when we have entered all the transactions up to our balance sheet date, we need to make various **adjustments** if the balance sheet is going to reflect the true financial position of the company.

Bear in mind always that a balance sheet is only a snapshot at a particular moment – a few seconds later it will be different, even if only slightly.

SBL's balance sheet

SBL made well over a hundred transactions in its first year. Rather than go through every one of them, I have summarised them so we have a manageable number. I have also identified the four adjustments we need to make [Table 2.1].

SILK BLOOMERS LIMITED

First-year transactions and adjustments

1   Issue shares for £10,000.
2   Borrow £10,000 from Sarah's parents.
3   Buy a car for £9,000.
4   Buy £8,000 worth of stock (cash on delivery).
5   Buy £20,000 worth of stock on credit.
6   Sell £6,000 worth of stock for £12,000 cash.
7   Sell £12,000 worth of stock for £30,000 on credit.
8   Rent equipment and buy stationery for £2,000 on credit.
9   Pay car running costs of £4,000.
10 Pay interest on loan of £1,000.
11 Collect £15,000 of cash from debtors.
12 Pay creditors £10,000.
13 Make a prepayment of £8,000 on account of stock.
14 Adjust for £2,000 of telephone expenses not yet billed.
15 Adjust for depreciation of fixed assets of £3,000.
16 Adjust for £4,000 expected tax liability.
17 Adjust for £3,000 dividend to be paid.

Table 2.1 Summary of SBL's first-year transactions and adjustments

Don't worry for the time being if you don't understand some of the things on this list – I will explain them as we go along.

What we are going to do is look at the effect each of these transactions and adjustments has on SBL's balance sheet. We will do this using the balance sheet chart as follows:

- We will draw one chart for each transaction or adjustment.

- Each chart will show two balance sheets – the balance sheet immediately before the transaction/adjustment and the balance sheet immediately after the transaction/adjustment.

- I will shade in the boxes that change due to each transaction or adjustment.

Transaction 1 – pay £10,000 cash into SBL's bank account as starting capital (share capital)

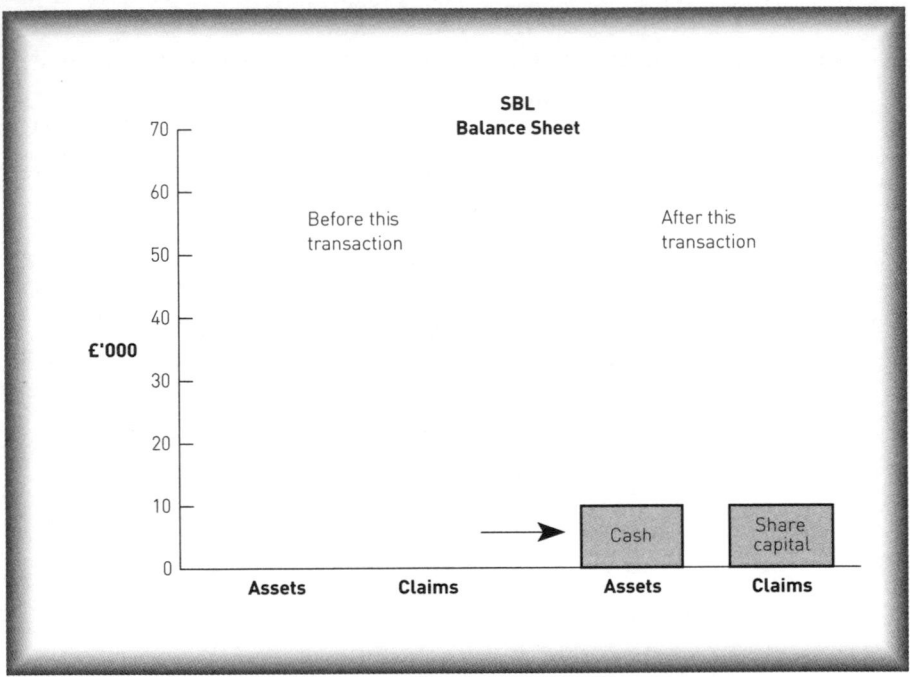

Figure 2.1

Before this transaction, SBL had no assets and therefore no claims over those (non-existent) assets.

The first thing Sarah did was to pay £10,000 of her own money into the company's bank account so that the company could commence operations. In return she received a certificate saying she owned 10,000 £1 shares in the company. Thus the company acknowledges that she has a claim over any net assets the company might have.

Since the company has no other assets or liabilities yet, the whole £10,000 must be 'owed' to the shareholders. Sarah, as the only shareholder, would claim it all.

To account for this transaction, we create a box on the assets bar called **cash** with a height of £10,000 and another box on the claims bar called **share capital**, also with a height of £10,000. This is SBL's balance sheet immediately after completion of this transaction.

Transaction 2 – SBL borrows £10,000 from Sarah's parents

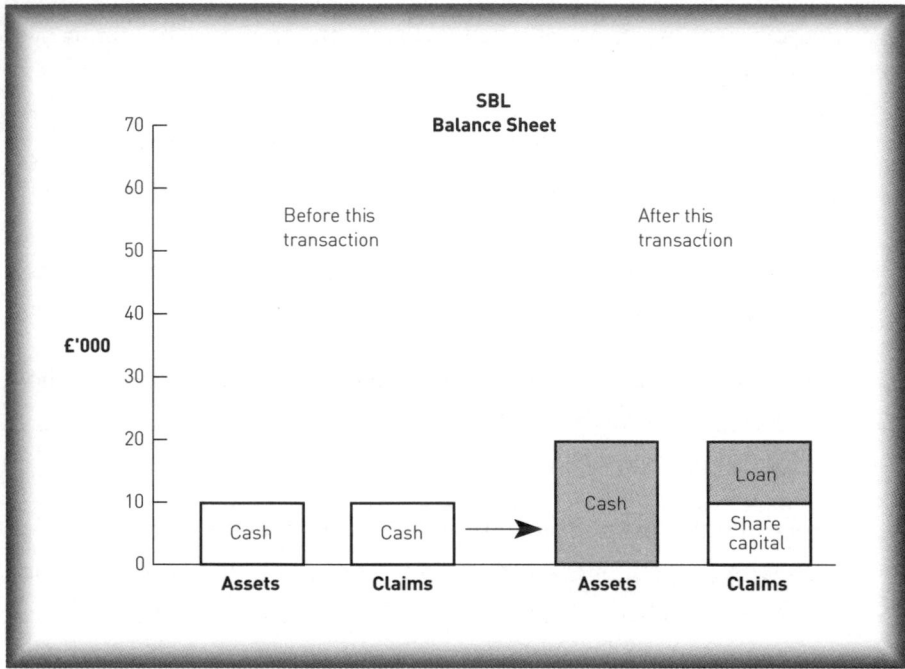

Figure 2.2

SBL needed more cash than Sarah could afford to invest herself, so she persuaded her parents to lend the company £10,000.

Immediately *before* this transaction, the balance sheet looks as it did immediately after the last transaction (with £10,000 of cash and £10,000 of share capital).

As a result of this transaction, the company has more cash in its bank account. Hence the cash box gets bigger by £10,000.

At the same time, however, a liability has been created. At some point the company will have to repay Sarah's parents the £10,000. They have said they will not ask for repayment for at least three years, so this is a **long-term loan**.

Notice two things:

- The two bars remain the same height.
- Sarah, as the shareholder, has not been made richer or poorer by this transaction – she still has a claim over £10,000 worth of the company's assets.

Transaction 3 – buy £9,000 of fixed assets (car)

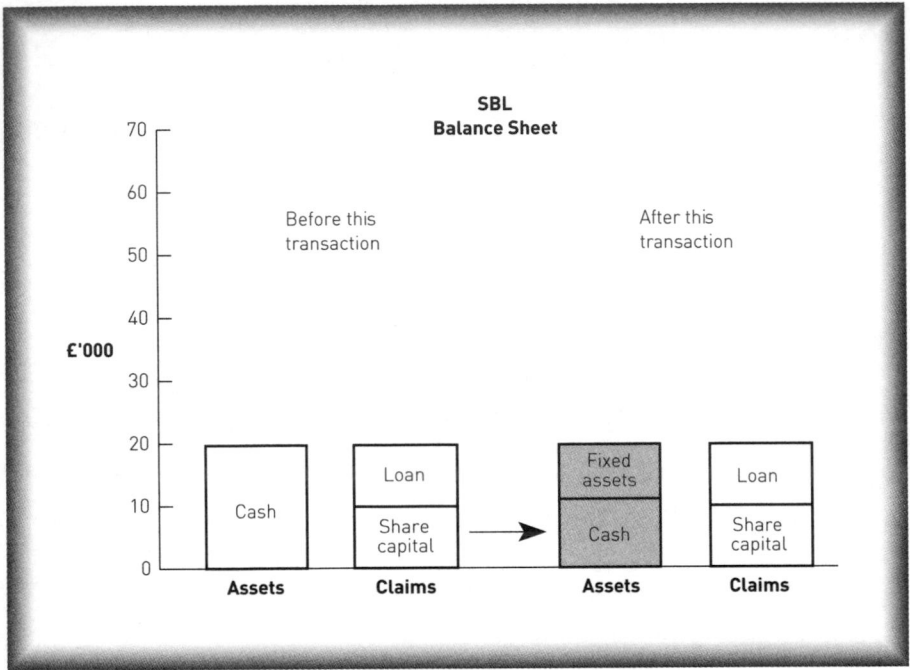

Figure 2.3

Before Sarah could start business, she needed a car to visit potential customers and deliver stock. This car cost SBL £9,000.

Since Sarah paid for the car in cash, the cash box must go down by £9,000. At the same time, SBL has acquired assets worth exactly £9,000. Hence, the company's total assets have not changed and the assets bar remains the same height.

No claim over the company's assets has been created or changed by this transaction, so the claims bar stays the same height as well. As always, the balance sheet remains in balance.

I didn't pay cash, actually, Chris; I paid with a cheque.

Yes, but, to an accountant, paying cash simply means paying at the time, as distinct from paying in, say, thirty days' time which many suppliers agree to. Paying by cheque or banker's draft means that the cash goes out of your bank account almost immediately, so we call that a cash payment.

Transaction 4 – buy £8,000 of stock (cash on delivery)

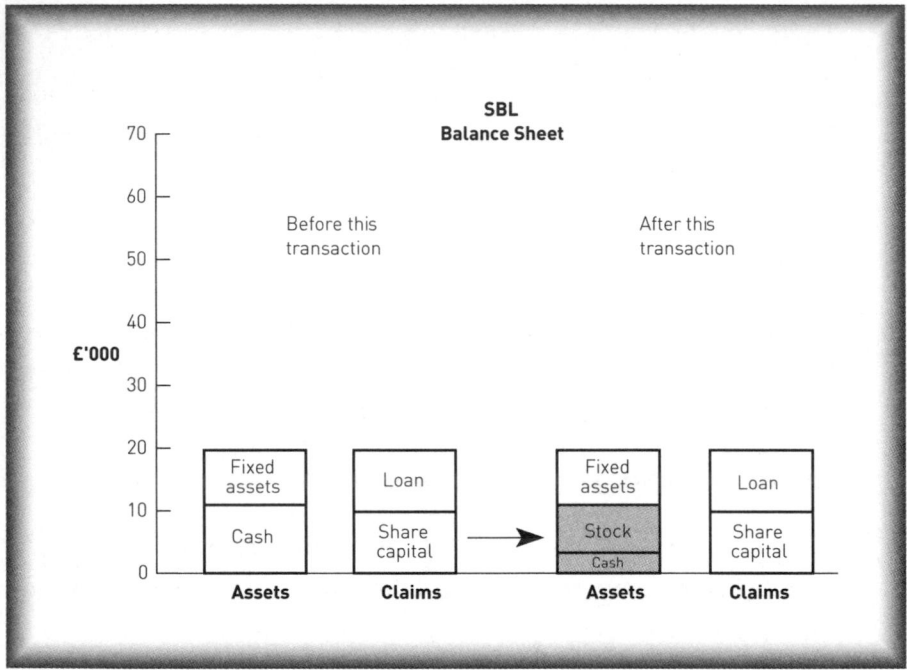

Figure 2.4

The first stock of silk flowers that Sarah bought had to be paid for at the time of purchase, as the supplier was nervous about SBL's ability to pay. This transaction is very similar to the previous one. The cash box goes down by another £8,000, but SBL has acquired another asset, **stock**, which is worth £8,000. Thus we create another box on the assets bar called stock with a height of £8,000. The bars therefore remain the same height.

Notice that we have made two entries on the balance sheet for every transaction so far. Obviously, if we change one box we must change another one to make the bars remain the same height.

If you have ever heard the term **double-entry book-keeping**, and wondered what it meant, you now know. It's exactly what we're doing when we change two boxes to enter a transaction. As you can see, there is nothing very difficult about it. The 'double entry' of transactions on a balance sheet is the way we apply the fundamental principle that the assets must always equal the claims.

Transaction 5 – buy £20,000 of stock (on credit)

Figure 2.5

Sarah subsequently persuaded her supplier to agree that SBL need not pay until sixty days after delivery of the stock. This gave her time to sell some of the stock and get some cash into the company's bank account (otherwise she would not have had enough money to pay for the stock!).

The stock bar therefore goes up by the amount of new stock (£20,000). This time, however, the cash bar does not change. Instead, we have created a liability to the supplier. The supplier has a claim over some of the assets of the company. Liabilities to suppliers are called **trade creditors**. Thus we create a new box on the claims bar called trade creditors with a height of £20,000.

Notice that, despite the transactions to date, nothing has been done which has made Sarah, as the shareholder, richer or poorer. Her claim over the company's assets is still what she put in as share capital, i.e. £10,000.

Transaction 6 – sell £6,000 of stock for £12,000 (cash on delivery)

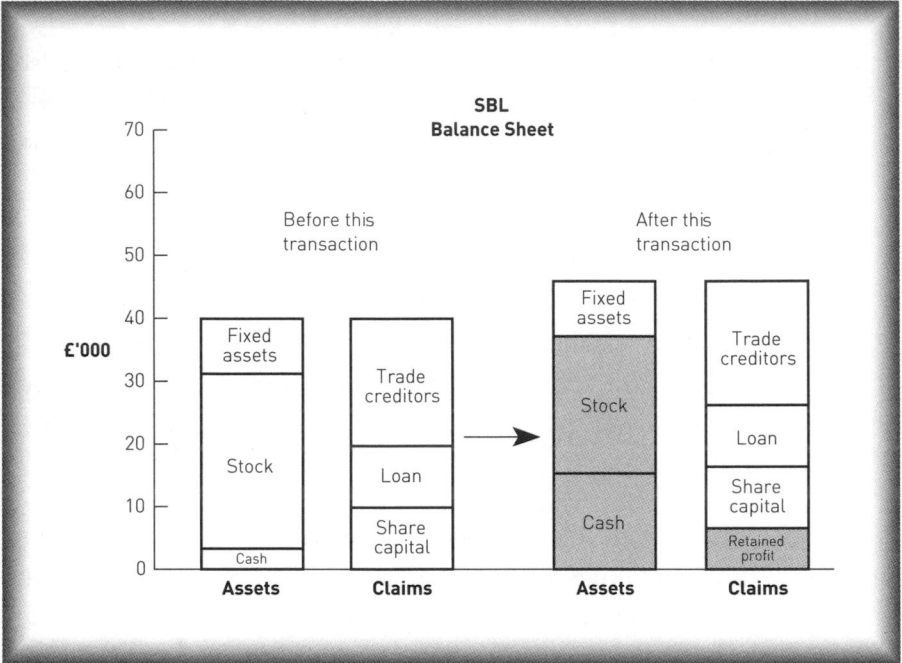

Figure 2.6

SBL sold, for £12,000 paid cash on delivery, stock which had only cost SBL £6,000. The £6,000 profit is not owed to anyone else, so it must belong to the shareholders. This, therefore, is a transaction which affects the shareholders' wealth.

The cash box goes up by £12,000 (since this is how much cash SBL received) and the stock box goes down by £6,000 (since this is the value of the stock sold). Hence the assets bar goes up by a net £6,000.

We create a new box on the claims bar called **retained profit** and give it a height of £6,000. This means the claims bar goes up by £6,000 and the balance sheet remains in balance.

You will remember that the claims of the shareholders ('shareholders' equity') are made up of the capital invested plus the retained profit. Shareholders' equity is therefore the £10,000 share capital Sarah put in plus the £6,000 retained profit from this transaction. SBL has done what companies exist to do: make their shareholders richer.

Transaction 7 – sell £12,000 of stock for £30,000 on credit

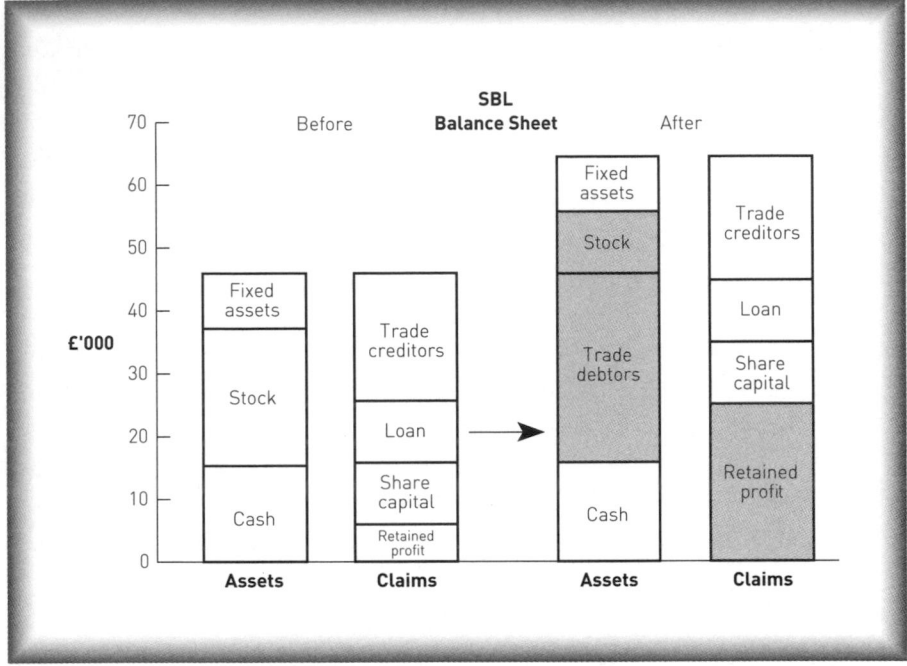

Figure 2.7

SBL subsequently sold £12,000 worth of stock for £30,000. The difference between this transaction and the last is that Sarah agreed that her customers need not pay immediately. Instead, she sent them invoices for later settlement.

In addition to the fundamental principle, there are two basic concepts that we apply when drawing up a set of accounts. One of these is known as the **accruals basis**. This means that any sales and purchases that a company makes are deemed to have taken place (i.e. are **recognised**) when the goods are handed over (or the services performed), not when the payment is made. Thus, as soon as SBL delivered the stock, we would say the sale had been made and enter it on the balance sheet, even though the customer had not yet paid.

I'm not sure I see why this matters, Chris.

It's a question of when we say the profit was made. It may be clearer with a simple example. Assume that on Monday you buy two tickets to a concert for £40. On Tuesday you sell them to a friend of yours for £50. You actually hand over the tickets to your friend on the Tuesday, but you agree that she need not pay you until Wednesday. On which of the three days would you say you had made the £10 profit?

Tuesday, I suppose.

Exactly, the day you handed over the goods. We use the same principle with companies to decide into which year the profit of a particular transaction goes.

Let's get back to SBL and see how we enter this transaction. We have to create a new box on the assets bar which we call **trade debtors**. This is what SBL is owed by the customers, so the box has a height of £30,000. The stock box must go down by £12,000, since this is the amount of stock that has been sold. The net impact is that the assets bar has gone up by £18,000, which is the profit on the transaction.

This £18,000 of profit (or extra assets) belongs to the shareholders, not to anyone else. Hence we increase retained profit by £18,000 and the two bars balance again.

Transaction 8 – rent equipment and buy stationery for £2,000 on credit

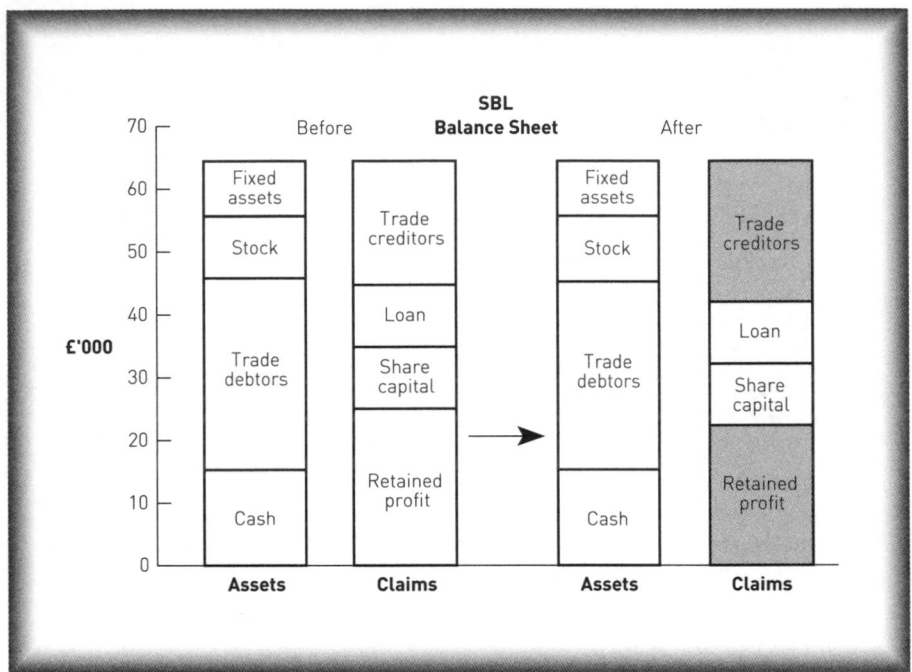

Figure 2.8

Sarah decided to rent the office equipment (word processor, fax, etc.) that she needed. She got all these things, as well as stationery etc. from a friend in the office supply business, who sent her a bill for £2,000 but agreed she could pay whenever she could afford it.

Since SBL didn't pay at the time of the transaction, its liabilities must have gone up by £2,000. Thus we increase the height of the trade creditors box by £2,000.

What, though, is the other balance sheet entry? We haven't actually bought the equipment so we can't call it a fixed asset and the stationery is more or less used up during the year.

These items are what we call the **expenses** of running the business. They reduce the profits made by selling stock and thus reduce the shareholders' wealth.

Our 'double entry' is therefore to reduce the retained profit box by £2,000, which makes our bars balance again.

Transaction 9 – pay car running costs of £4,000 in cash

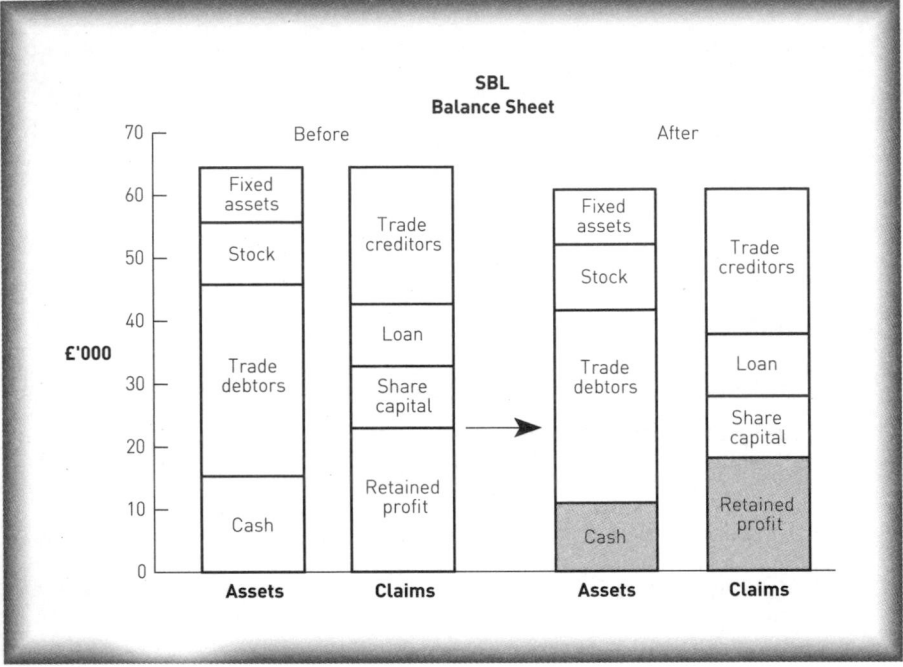

Figure 2.9

Sarah had to pay for petrol, servicing, etc. on the car. These were all paid in cash.

Clearly, as a result of this transaction, the cash box must go down by £4,000. This money is gone for ever. This transaction therefore represents another expense of the business. Consequently, the shareholders are poorer and we reduce retained profit by £4,000.

Transaction 10 – pay £1,000 interest on long-term loan

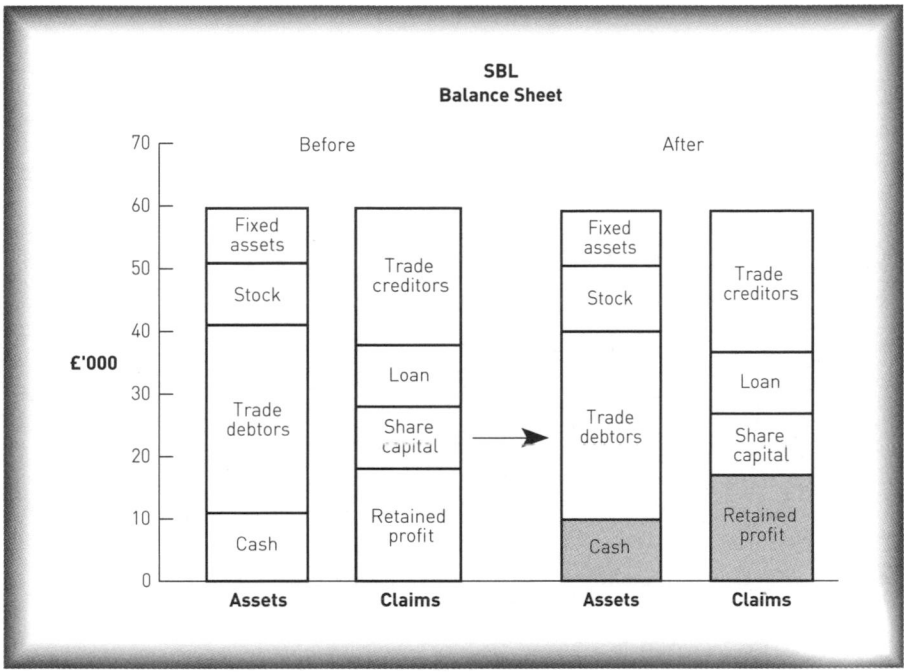

Figure 2.10

Sarah's parents generously said they would not ask SBL to repay their loan for at least three years. They do, however, want some interest. Sarah agreed that SBL would pay them 10 per cent per year. Thus SBL paid £1,000 in interest at the end of the year.

This was paid in cash so the cash box goes down again by £1,000, and once again it is the poor old shareholder who suffers: retained profit goes down by £1,000.

Transaction 11 – collect £15,000 cash from debtors

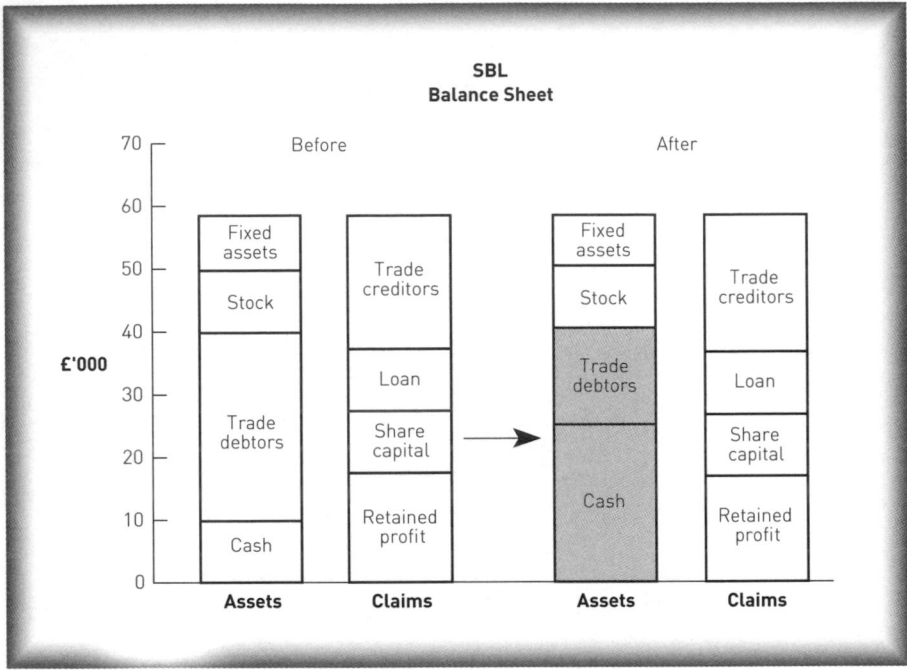

Figure 2.11

As we have already seen, in the course of the year, Sarah sold stock for £30,000 to be paid for at a later date. We accounted for this in Transaction 7. Later in the year, she actually collected £15,000 of the £30,000 owed by her customers.

The entries for this transaction are very straightforward. The cash box goes up by £15,000 and the trade debtors box down by £15,000.

Notice that retained profit is not affected by this transaction. We recognised the profit on the sale of these goods when the goods were delivered (Transaction 7). In this transaction we have merely collected some of the cash from that transaction.

Transaction 12 – pay £10,000 cash to creditors

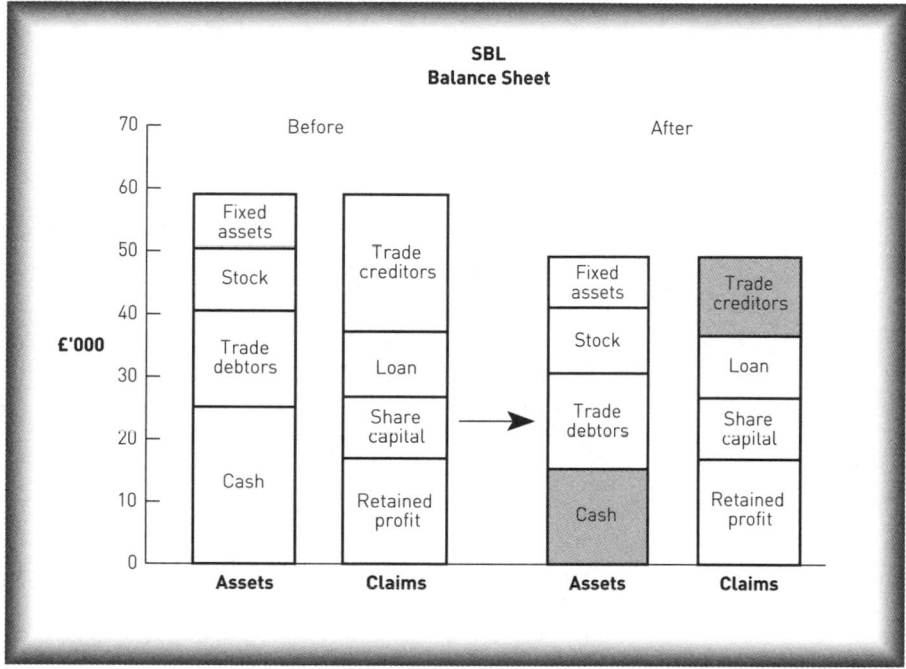

Figure 2.12

In the same way that Sarah sold stock on credit, she also bought £22,000 of stock and other goods on credit. Obviously, these things have to be paid for eventually and, during the first year, £10,000 was paid out to creditors.

The cash box goes down by £10,000 and the trade creditors box goes down by £10,000 since the company now owes less than before.

As with collecting cash from trade debtors, there is no impact on profit due to this transaction.

Transaction 13 – make a prepayment of £8,000 for stock

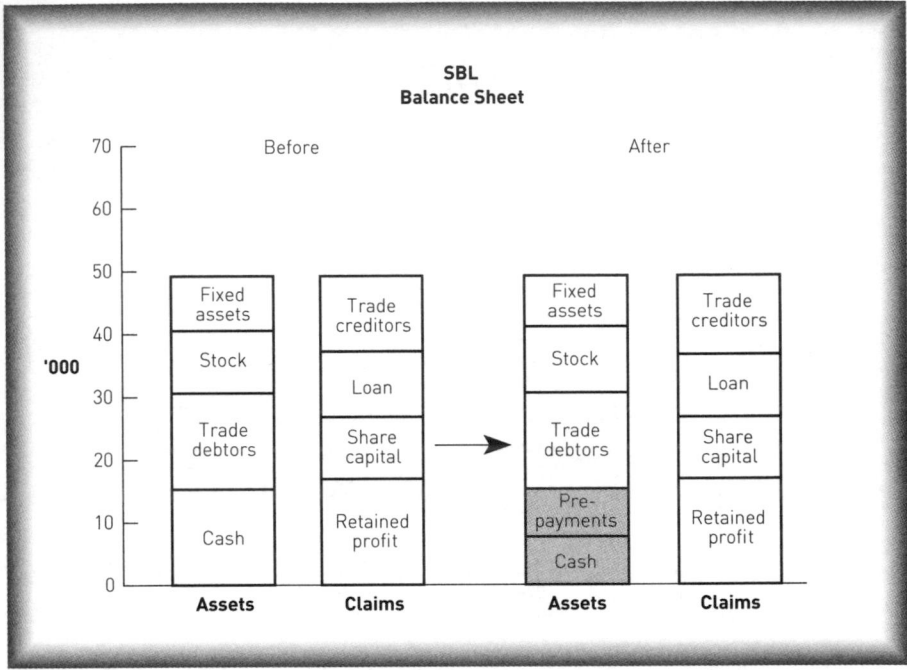

Figure 2.13

Towards the end of the year, Sarah paid a new supplier in advance for some stock. This stock had not been delivered by the balance sheet date.

Clearly, the cash box goes down again by £8,000 since SBL actually paid out this much cash. What, though, is the other entry?

Are the shareholders richer or poorer as a result of this transaction? The answer is no, because, although SBL has paid out £8,000 in cash, the company is owed £8,000 worth of stock. This is an asset to SBL.

Thus we create a new box on the assets bar called **prepayments** with a height of £8,000. This says that the company is owed goods with a value of £8,000.

Once again, the balance sheet balances.

Adjustment 14 – adjust for £2,000 telephone expenses not yet billed

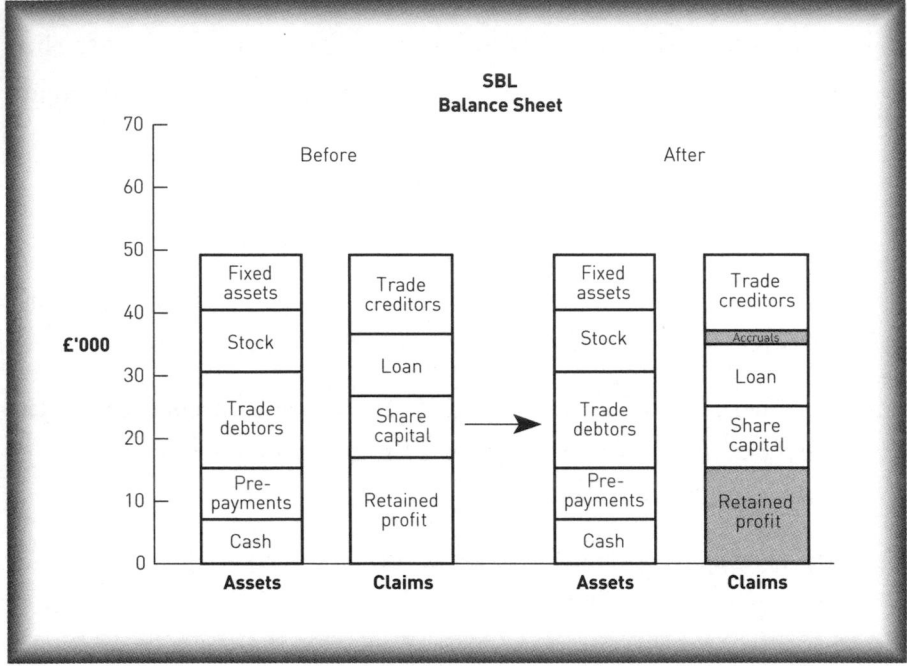

Figure 2.14

Thanks to a mix-up in administration, SBL has not received a bill for its telephone and fax usage for the year. We know, however, that a bill will appear sooner or later and Sarah estimates that it will be for around £2,000.

We included sales in our balance sheet even when they were not paid for at the time of delivery. This is what I called the 'accruals basis' of accounting. The other aspect of the accruals basis is that we must include all the costs involved in making those sales. This is known as **matching**. In this case, we know that telephone expenses have been incurred to achieve the sales we have already recognised in the accounts. Thus, under the matching principle, we must recognise these expenses even though the bill has not arrived.

We therefore reduce retained profit by £2,000 and create a box on the claims bar called **accruals** with a height of £2,000.

Accruals are any costs you haven't been billed for, but know you will have to pay and which have to be recognised under the matching principle.

Adjustment 15 – adjust for £3,000 depreciation of fixed assets

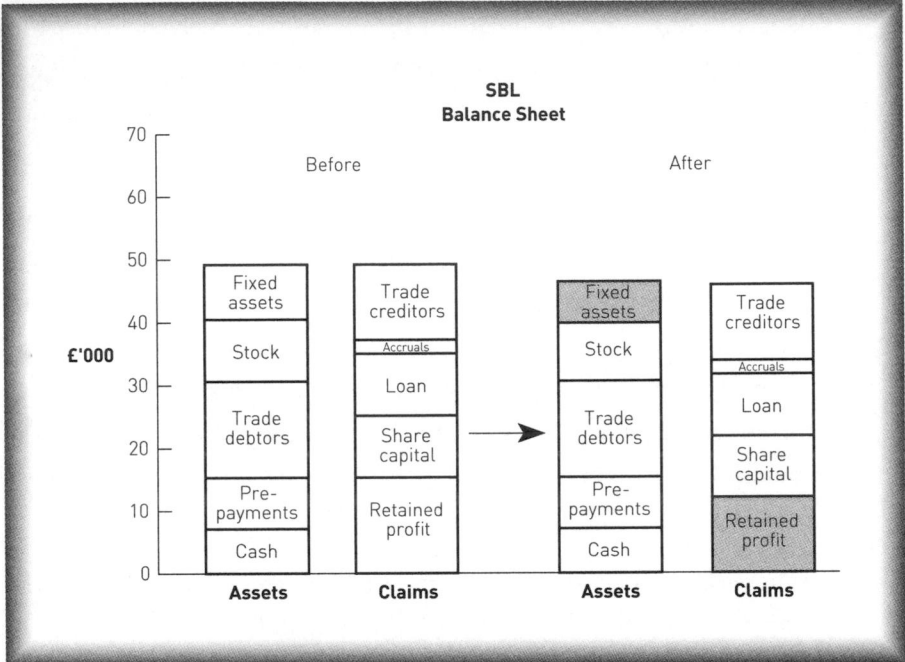

Figure 2.15

When Sarah bought the car, we put it on the balance sheet at the price she paid for it. Since Sarah has been using the car to visit customers during the year, its value will have declined, i.e. it will have **depreciated**. This effectively means that the shareholders have become poorer because, if all the assets were sold off, there would be less cash for the shareholders.

In other words, there is a cost to the shareholders of Sarah using the car. Under the matching principle we need to allow for this cost in the accounts.

The way we do this is as follows:

- We put the asset on the balance sheet initially at the price the company paid for it (as we did in Transaction 3).
- We then decide what we think the useful life of the asset is.
- We then gradually reduce the value of the asset over that period (i.e. we depreciate it).

In SBL's case, assume the car has a useful life of three years. If we also assume that it will lose its value steadily over that period, then at the end of one year it will have lost a third of its value, i.e. it will have gone down from £9,000 to £6,000.

We therefore reduce the fixed assets box by this amount. If an asset has lost some value, the shareholders must have become poorer, so again we reduce the retained profit by £3,000.

The value of an asset on a balance sheet is known as the net book value.

Note that this is not necessarily what you could get for the asset if you sold it: it is the cost of the asset less the total depreciation on the asset to date.

Adjustment 16 – adjust for £4,000 expected tax liability

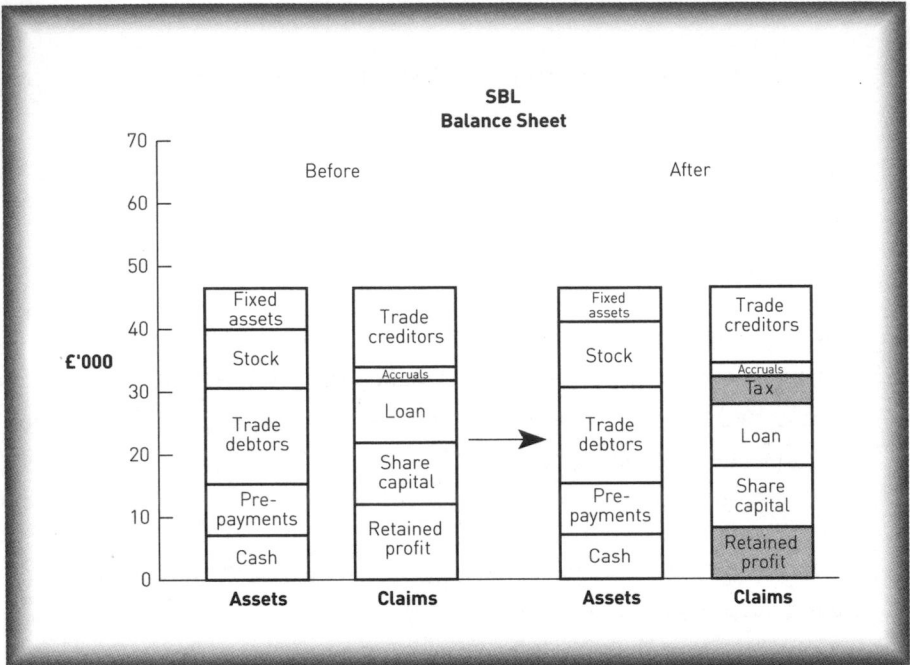

Figure 2.16

Unfortunately, SBL is going to have to pay some corporation tax, which is the tax payable on companies' profits. Tax is not easy to calculate accurately, because the Inland Revenue has complicated rules. We can make an estimate, though, and I would think that £4,000 will be fairly close.

We thus create a box called **tax** (more accurate, perhaps, would be **corporation tax liability**) with a height of £4,000.

The other entry is again retained profit, since the £4,000 would otherwise have belonged to the shareholders. Paying tax makes the shareholders poorer.

Adjustment 17 – adjust for £3,000 dividend to be paid

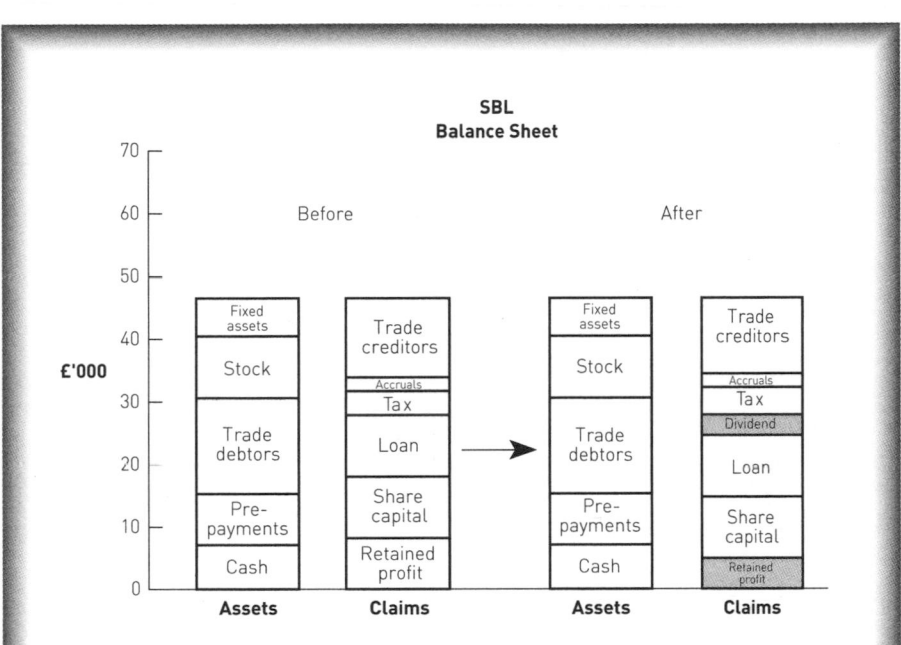

Figure 2.17

At the end of the year, although she had not drawn up proper accounts, Sarah knew that she had made a small profit. As the company had some cash in the bank, she therefore decided, as a shareholder, that the company should pay a dividend. Although she decided to do this, SBL had not actually paid the cash out at the year end. At the year end, therefore, SBL owed the shareholders (i.e. Sarah) £3,000 for the dividend.

This transaction is identical to the tax accrual. We create a box with a height of £3,000 called **dividend** (again, **dividend liability** would be a more accurate description).

A dividend is simply the shareholders taking out of the company some of the profits that the company has made. Thus retained profit must go down by £3,000.

So the box you have been calling 'retained profit' all this time is really all the profit the company has made less what is paid out to the shareholders. Hence the term 'retained' profit?

Exactly. And that, you will be glad to hear, is it. That's our last balance sheet entry done. The final balance sheet [Figure 2.17] is SBL's balance sheet at the end of the year.

The different forms of balance sheet

OK, so we've got the balance sheet chart. How do I turn that into something I can show my accountants?

There are two common layouts of a balance sheet, although they are both essentially the same.

The 'American' balance sheet

As you will recall, our balance sheet chart is based on the balance sheet equation:

$$
\begin{aligned}
\text{Assets} \ &= \ \text{Claims} \\
&= \ \text{Liabilities + Shareholders' equity}
\end{aligned}
$$

We can simply lay out our balance sheet according to this equation [Table 2.2]. This is literally just the 'numbers version' of our balance sheet chart. We list all the assets and total them up. Below that we list all the claims. The only difference between this and the balance sheet chart is that I have listed the assets and claims under the category headings that I talked about when we first looked at Wingate's balance sheet. This format is used by virtually all American companies.

SILK BLOOMERS LIMITED

Final balance sheet – American style

		£'000
Assets		
Fixed assets		6.0
Current assets		
Stock	10.0	
Prepayments	8.0	
Trade debtors	15.0	
Cash	7.0	
Total current assets		40.0
Total assets		46.0
Claims		
Current liabilities		
Trade creditors	12.0	
Accruals	2.0	
Tax payable	4.0	
Dividends payable	3.0	
Total current liabilities		21.0
Long-term liabilities		10.0
Shareholders' equity		
Share capital	10.0	
Retained profit	5.0	
Total shareholders' equity		15.0
Total claims		46.0

Table 2.2 SBL's balance sheet: American style

The 'British' balance sheet

As you will remember, we can rearrange the balance sheet equation to look like this:

$$\text{Assets} - \text{Liabilities} = \text{Shareholders' equity}$$

This equation is the basis of British and many European balance sheets. The attraction of this layout is that it displays more clearly the net assets of the company and how those net assets were attained [Table 2.3]. Of course, none of the individual assets or liabilities has changed.

The other thing you would normally do is to put the previous year's balance sheet alongside the current year's so they can be compared. Since SBL didn't exist last year, there's no balance sheet to show. If you look at Wingate's balance sheet on page 279, however, you will see that it is laid out in the British style and has the previous year's figures alongside this year's.

Basic concepts of accounting

As I mentioned earlier, in addition to the fundamental principle, there are two basic concepts that we always apply when drawing up a set of accounts. These concepts are:

- **The accruals basis and matching**
- **The going concern assumption**

SILK BLOOMERS LIMITED

Final balance sheet – British style

	£'000
Net assets	
Fixed assets	6.0
Current assets	
Stock	10.0
Prepayments	8.0
Trade debtors	15.0
Cash	7.0
	40.0
Current liabilities	
Trade creditors	(12.0)
Accruals	(2.0)
Tax payable	(4.0)
Dividends payable	(3.0)
	(21.0)
Long-term liabilities	(10.0)
Net assets	15.0
Shareholders' equity	
Share capital	10.0
Retained profit	5.0
Total	15.0

Table 2.3 SBL's balance sheet: British style

The accruals basis and matching

We discussed this when looking at SBL. To summarise it:

- Revenue is recognised when it is earned, not when cash is received; expenses are recognised when they are incurred, not when cash is paid.

- Expenses are matched with the revenues they have generated so that the retained profit reflects the profit earned by the company over the relevant period.

The going concern assumption

Go back to when we first started discussing balance sheets. We agreed that shareholders' equity is what the shareholders of a company would get if the company sold all the assets and paid off all its liabilities.

This is a nice, simple way of looking at a balance sheet to understand what it is saying. In practice, however, if a company were to stop trading and try to sell its assets, it may not get as much for some of them as their value on the balance sheet. For example:

- When a company stops trading, it can be very hard to persuade debtors to pay.

- Fixed assets may not have the same value to anyone else as they do to the company.

Accounts are therefore drawn up on the basis that the company is a **going concern**, i.e. that it is not about to cease trading.

Let's now recap quickly before going on to look at the P&L and cash flow statement.

SUMMARY

- The balance sheet shows a company's financial position at any given moment.

- Every transaction a company makes will affect its financial position and must therefore be recorded on the balance sheet.

- In addition, various adjustments are usually required before a balance sheet accurately reflects a company's financial position.

- All balance sheet entries are made using 'double entry' so that the balance sheet always balances.

- There are two basic concepts which apply to all properly drawn up balance sheets:
  - the accruals basis and matching
  - the going concern assumption.

In this session, all I am going to do is explain what the P&L and cash flow statement are.

CHAPTER 3

The profit & loss account and cash flow statement

- The profit & loss account
- The cash flow statement
- 'Definitive' vs 'descriptive' statements
- Summary

Now we know what a balance sheet is and how to construct one, we can move on to the P&L and cash flow statement. In this session, all I am going to do is explain what the P&L and cash flow statement are. We'll see how to construct them in our next session.

The profit & loss account

Let's start by looking at a hypothetical situation relating to an individual's P&L. Assume you're a fortune-hunter, Tom, after Sarah for her money. What would you want to know before asking her to marry you?

How rich she is or, as you would say, what her net worth is.

So if I told you that her net worth today is £25,000, and added that it was only £20,000 this time last year, what would you think of her as a target for your 'affections'?

Not a great deal.

Which could just be one of your bigger mistakes, Tom. We know Sarah's net worth has gone up by £5,000 over the last year. There are many ways that could have happened. Here are two very different ones:

- It could be that Sarah earned a total of £15,000 during the year and spent £10,000 of this on food, drink, holidays, tax, etc. The remaining £5,000 she saved, either by spending it on real assets or by putting it in her bank deposit account. Add these savings to the £20,000 net worth she had at the start of the year and you get her net worth today of £25,000.

- An alternative scenario is that, a year ago, Sarah landed an extremely well-paid job, earning £500,000 a year. She's quite extravagant, but in a normal year could only have spent (including a lot of tax) £245,000 of this income on herself. She should, therefore, have saved £255,000. Unfortunately, during the year she had to pay an American hospital for a series of operations for her brother. He's better now, but the operations cost her a total of £250,000. As a result, she only saved £5,000 during the year.

What would you feel about Sarah in each of those situations, Tom?

I'd obviously write her off in the first case. In the second, I'd be more than a little interested, provided she didn't have any more sick relatives.

Exactly. My point is that, as well as knowing what Sarah's net worth is and by how much it has changed since last year, an explanation of why she only got £5,000 richer during the year can be very important. If we're going to make a sensible judgment about a company's future performance, we need a similar explanation. This is what a P&L gives you.

If you look at the bottom of Wingate's balance sheet on page 279, you will see that the company's retained profit (its 'savings') rose by £268k during the year from £2,178k to £2,446k. If you look on page 278, you will see Wingate's P&L, the penultimate line of which shows retained profit in year five of £268k. This is not a coincidence. The P&L is just giving you more detail about how and why the retained profit item on the balance sheet changed over the last year. That's all there is to it.

The cash flow statement

Let's now go back to your fortune hunting for a moment, Tom. Suppose you have discovered that Sarah's current net worth is actually £10m, having risen from £9m this time last year. You have seen the equivalent of her P&L which shows that this rise in her net wealth is due to all the interest on money in various deposit accounts. In short, you expect this increase in her already vast wealth to continue. How would you feel about her?

I'd be down to the jewellers in a flash, although I have the feeling you're going to tell me that would be a mistake.

I'm afraid so. Let me give you some more information about Sarah. Most of her money is tied up in a 'trust' set up for her by her wealthy grandparents. All the interest on this money is kept in the trust as well. Although Sarah is the beneficiary of the trust and therefore owns all the assets in it, she is not allowed access to them for another ten years. Meanwhile she's more or less out of ready cash and is going to be penniless for those ten years.

How would you feel if you married her and *then* learned about this situation, Tom?

Sick as a parrot, I imagine.

Precisely. My point this time is that an individual or a company can be rich and getting richer, but at the same time the cash they have to spend in the short term can be running out. However rich you are, you can't survive without cash to spend.

I take the point, but I don't quite see how this would happen to a company.

Take SBL as an example. In Transaction 7, SBL sold stock for £30,000 but agreed that the customers need not pay for a while. As we saw, this

made the shareholders richer, but did not immediately bring in any cash. Later, in Transaction 11, some of this cash was collected. If it hadn't been, though, and SBL had still been obliged to pay its suppliers, SBL would have run out of cash completely.

Far more small companies go out of business through running out of cash than by being inherently unprofitable.

If we look at a company's balance sheets, we can see how the cash balance changed over the period between the balance sheet dates. The cash flow statement merely explains how and why the cash changed as it did.

I hear what you say, Chris, but look at Wingate's cash flow statement on page 280. This shows a reduction in cash during the year of £285k. But the balance sheet on page 279 shows cash going down by only £5k from £20k to £15k.

What you say is right, but there is a simple explanation. In accounting terms, an overdraft is like a negative amount of cash. It's no different from your own current account really. You either have a positive balance or you are in overdraft, i.e. you have a negative amount of cash. As it happens, Wingate had two bank accounts. One had a positive balance in it, the other was in overdraft. You can see the overdraft detailed in Note 12 of the accounts on page 285. The cash flow statement shows the total cash change of both of these, so what you have is as follows:

- At the end of year four, Wingate had cash of £20k and an overdraft of £613k, making a net overdraft of £593k.

- At the end of year five, Wingate had cash of £15k and an overdraft of £893k, making a net overdraft of £878k.

- The difference between these net overdraft figures is £285k, which is what the cash flow statement shows cash going down by.

'Definitive' vs 'descriptive' statements

Let's just summarise what we know about the three key statements in a set of accounts.

- The balance sheet tells us what the assets and liabilities of a company are at a point in time.

- The P&L tells us how and why the retained profit of the company changed over the course of the last year.

- The cash flow statement tells us how and why the cash/overdraft of the company changed over the last year.

The balance sheet is thus the **definitive** statement of a company's financial position. It tells us absolutely where a company stands at any given moment. The P&L and cash flow statement provide extremely important information but, nonetheless, they are only **descriptive** statements: they describe how certain balance sheet items changed during the year.

We could easily draw up statements to show how other balance sheet items changed, if we wanted to. In fact, the notes to Wingate's accounts do this. Look, for example, at the balance sheet on page 279. This shows that fixed assets went up from £4,445k at the end of year four to £5,326k at the end of year five. If you look at Note 9 on page 284, you will see that it consists of a table, the bottom right-hand corner of which shows these two figures.

This table is merely a descriptive statement of how and why the fixed assets figure has changed over the last year. The only reason the P&L and cash flow statement are given such prominence in the annual report is because they are so important.

All of this presumably explains why you insisted on starting with the balance sheet.

Yes. As I said earlier, the balance sheet is the fundamental principle of accounting put into practice. The balance sheet's role as the core of the accounting system is the single most important thing to understand about accounting. In fact, if you really understand a balance sheet and double entry, everything else about accounting suddenly becomes very simple.

If you ever find yourself confused about how to account for a transaction, the first thing you should do is look at the impact on the balance sheet. Then, if the transaction affects retained profit, you know it affects the P&L; if it affects cash, you know it affects the cash flow statement.

What you need to know now is how we draw up the P&L and cash flow statement. Before doing that though, let's just pause for another summary.

SUMMARY

- The balance sheet is the definitive statement of a company's financial position. It tells you what a company's assets and liabilities are at a point in time and hence what the company's net assets are. It also tells you how the company came by those net assets.

- The P&L is a descriptive statement. It tells you how and why the retained profit item on the balance sheet changed over the course of the last year.

- The cash flow statement is also a descriptive statement. It tells you how and why the cash/overdraft as shown on the balance sheet changed over the course of the last year.

- You can draw up descriptive statements for any other item on the balance sheet. The only reason that the P&L and cash flow statement are given such prominence in an annual report is because they describe the most important aspects of a business.

I'll start by showing you the P&L at its most simplistic and then we'll modify it slightly to make it more useful. We'll then repeat the same exercise for the cash flow statement.

Creating the profit & loss account and cash flow statement

- Creating the profit & loss account
- Creating the cash flow statement
- Summary

Now we're clear about what the P&L and cash flow statement are, we need to see how they are created. First we'll look at the P&L. I'll start by showing you the P&L at its most simplistic and then we'll modify it slightly to make it more useful. We'll then repeat the same exercise for the cash flow statement.

Creating the profit & loss account

The P&L as a list

Of the seventeen entries processed to get the balance sheet of SBL, only nine affected the retained profit of the company. These nine entries are shown in Table 4.1. Against each entry I have put the amount by which it affected retained profit. Entries that decrease retained profit are in brackets. As you can see the net effect on retained profit of all nine entries is £5,000.

From the balance sheet we know that the retained profit of SBL rose from zero to £5,000 in the course of the year. As we saw in the last chapter, a P&L merely shows how the retained profit changed over a period of time. The list in Table 4.1 shows exactly that: this is your P&L. What could be simpler than that?

Not a lot, I agree, but this doesn't look anything like Wingate's P&L.

You're right, it doesn't. That's because this P&L has two contradictory problems. On the one hand, it is too detailed. Most companies have hundreds or thousands of transactions in a year. It would be totally impracticable to list them all and very few people would have the time or inclination to read such a list anyway. What we do, therefore, is to group the transactions into a few simple categories to present a summary picture.

On the other hand, the P&L in Table 4.1 is not detailed enough. It shows that SBL made a profit of £24,000 on selling stock (Transactions

---

SILK BLOOMERS LIMITED

Entries affecting retained profit during first year

Entry number	Transaction/Adjustment	Impact on retained profit £'000
6	Sell stock (for cash)	6.0
7	Sell stock (invoiced)	18.0
8	Equipment rental etc.	(2.0)
9	Pay car expenses	(4.0)
10	Interest on loan	(1.0)
14	Telephone expenses accrued	(2.0)
15	Depreciation of fixed assets	(3.0)
16	Accrue tax	(4.0)
17	Accrue dividend	(3.0)
	Total	5.0

Note: The numbers in brackets are negative, i.e. they reduce retained profit

Table 4.1 Entries which affected SBL's retained profit

6 and 7). What it does not show is how much stock SBL had to sell to make that profit. For all we know, SBL might have sold £500,000 worth of stock for £524,000, or, alternatively, £6,000 worth of stock for £30,000. The impact on retained profit would be exactly the same.

If you look back at Transactions 6 and 7 [pages 30–33] you will see that, in fact, SBL sold a total of £18,000 worth of stock for £42,000.

A more useful P&L

We therefore re-write the above P&L as shown in Table 4.2.

Notice the following things about it:

- We show the total value of sales during the year (£42,000) as well as the total cost of the products sold (£18,000). The difference between these two (24,000) we call **gross profit**. Gross profit is the amount by which the sales of products affect the retained profit.

- We then take all the **operating expenses** and group them into categories. By operating expenses we mean any expenses related to the operations of the company which are not already included in cost of goods sold. We exclude anything to do with the funding of the company. Thus interest, tax and dividends, which all depend on the way the company is funded, are non-operating items. In SBL's case, the operating expense categories are 'Selling & distribution' (made up of car expenses and depreciation) and 'Administration' (made up of equipment rental, stationery and telephone expenses).

- The profit after these operating expenses we therefore call **operating profit**, which in SBL's case is £13,000.

- Sarah's parents then take their interest (£1,000), leaving **profit before tax** ('PBT') of £12,000.

- Profit before tax is effectively all the profit that is left over for the shareholders after paying the interest to the lenders (Sarah's

SILK BLOOMERS LIMITED

First year profit & loss account

		£'000
Sales		42.0
Cost of goods sold		(18.0)
Gross profit		24.0
Operating expenses		
Selling & distribution	(7.0)	
Administration	(4.0)	
		(11.0)
Operating profit		13.0
Interest payable		(1.0)
Profit before tax		12.0
Tax payable		(4.0)
Profit after tax		8.0
Dividend payable		(3.0)
Retained profit		5.0

Table 4.2 SBL's profit & loss account in first year of trading

parents, in this case) As with individuals' income, however, the Inland Revenue want their share of a company's profits before the shareholders get anything. We thus deduct tax of £4,000.

- This leaves **profit after tax** ('PAT') which is all due to the shareholders. Some of this is paid out to the shareholders as dividends (£3,000). What is then left (£5,000) is the retained profit.

Isn't the term 'profit & loss account' slightly misleading, Chris? As I see it, the P&L shows the profit the company has made for the shareholders, which is the profit after tax. Then some of that profit is distributed to the shareholders as a dividend; the dividend is nothing to do with the profit or loss of the company.

I would agree with you. It would probably be more accurate to call the P&L the 'statement of retained profit', or something similar.

Creating the cash flow statement

The cash flow statement as a list

Of the seventeen entries we made on SBL's balance sheet, ten affected the amount of cash the company had at the end of the year. These are shown in Table 4.3. Four of these entries increased the amount of cash the company had; the other six (shown in brackets again) decreased the cash balance. The net effect of these ten entries was to increase cash between the start and end of the year by £7,000.

From the balance sheet, we know that the cash in the company rose from zero to £7,000 during the year. The statement in Table 4.3 just shows how this happened. This is your cash flow statement.

As with the P&L, this list would become very long and not very informative for companies of significant size. Again, we can improve the situation by grouping the entries under six different headings, as shown in Table 4.4.

SILK BLOOMERS LIMITED

Entries affecting cash during first year

Entry number	Transaction/Adjustment	Impact on cash £'000
1	Issue shares	10.0
2	Borrow from parents	10.0
3	Buy fixed assets for cash	(9.0)
4	Buy stock for cash	(8.0)
6	Sell stock for cash	12.0
9	Pay car expenses	(4.0)
10	Interest on loan	(1.0)
11	Collect cash from debtors	15.0
12	Pay creditors	(10.0)
13	Pay for stock in advance	(8.0)
	Total	7.0

Note: As with the P&L, the numbers in brackets are negative, i.e. they reduce the amount of cash that the company has

Table 4.3 Entries which affected SBL's cash flow

- **Operating activities** consist of all items that relate to the company's operations. In SBL's case this included buying and selling stock, paying expenses, collecting cash in from debtors and paying cash out both to creditors, and as a prepayment for stock.

- **Returns on investments and servicing of finance** means the interest paid on loans and any dividends or interest received on investments or cash that the company has on deposit. In SBL's case, we have just the £1,000 interest payment on the loan from Sarah's parents.

SILK BLOOMERS LIMITED

Cash flow statement for first year

		£'000
Operating activities		
Buy stock for cash	(8.0)	
Sell stock for cash	12.0	
Pay car expenses	(4.0)	
Collect cash from debtors	15.0	
Pay creditors	(10.0)	
Pay for stock in advance	(8.0)	
		(3.0)
Returns on investments and servicing of finance		
Interest payable on loan		(1.0)
Taxation		
Total		0.0
Capital expenditure		
Purchase of fixed assets		(9.0)
Equity dividends paid		
Total		0.0
Financing		
Shares issued	10.0	
Loan from Sarah's parents	10.0	
		20.0
Net change in cash balance		7.0

Table 4.4 SBL's cash flow statement in first year of trading

- **Taxation** is the tax on the profits of the company. In SBL's case, the tax was accrued but had not actually been paid. Hence there is no impact on cash.

- **Capital expenditure** includes all buying and selling of fixed assets which enable the operating activities to take place. In SBL's case, this was just the purchase of a car.

- **Equity dividends paid** is the dividends paid out to shareholders. As with the tax, the dividend Sarah decided to pay herself, although 'accrued' (i.e. allowed for) at the date of the balance sheet, had not actually been paid. Hence, no cash went out of the company.

- **Financing** consists of all transactions relating to the raising of funds to operate the business. In SBL's case, this meant issuing some shares to Sarah in return for cash and borrowing more cash from her parents.

Drawing up a cash flow statement under these headings does make it easier to understand quickly where the cash in the business has come from and gone to. The operating activities section, however, is normally written in a different way. To understand this, we have to consider the relationship between profit and cash flow.

Profit and cash flow

Let's suppose you decide to sell flowers (real ones this time) from a stall on the pavement. You'd go down to the market at the crack of dawn and pay cash there and then for your flowers. You would then set up your stall on the pavement and sell the flowers for cash to any passing customers. If, on one particular day, you bought £100 worth of flowers at the market and sold them for a total of £150, you would have made a profit on the day of £50. Your cash flow on the day would also be £50, as you would have £50 more cash at the end of the day than you had at the start.

Now consider a completely different situation. Assume that on Monday you buy a £2 phone card. On Tuesday a friend asks you to make an urgent phone call for him. You use up all the units on the card. Your friend agrees to pay you £3 on Wednesday (which he duly does).

Let's now look at your profit and cash flow on each of the three days:

[£]	Monday	Tuesday	Wednesday	Total
Profit	0	1	0	1
Cash flow	(2)	0	3	1

On Monday you have to pay out £2 to buy the card, but it is still an asset worth £2 so you haven't made a profit or a loss. At the end of Monday, therefore, your cash is down by £2, but your profit is zero.

On Tuesday, you provide a service to your friend for £3. The cost of providing this service is the depreciation in value of the phonecard, which goes from being worth £2 to zero. Your profit on the day is therefore £1. Your cash flow, however, is zero, because you neither paid out nor received any cash.

On Wednesday, you receive the promised £3, so your cash flow is £3, although your profit is zero.

There are two things you should notice about this:

- **Profit and cash flow on any one day are not the same.** Similarly, with most businesses, profit and cash flow are not the same in any particular year (or month, etc.).

- **Over the three days, profit and cash flow are the same.** Similarly, with businesses, total profit and total cash flow will be the same in the long run. The difference between them is just a matter of timing.

These observations form the basis of a different cash flow statement. What we do is start out by saying that cash flow should equal profit and then adjust the figure to show why it didn't.

This version of the SBL cash flow statement is shown in Table 4.5. All the sections of this cash flow statement are identical to the previous one except 'Operating activities'. The first line of this section, as you can see, is operating profit. The rest of the section consists of the adjustments we have to make to operating profit to get the cash flow due to the operating activities. Let's look at each of these adjustments in turn.

Impact of depreciation on cash flow

The first adjustment is £3k of depreciation which we included to allow for the fact that the fixed assets had been 'used up' during the year. Depreciation therefore affects operating profit. It does not, however, affect cash. Hence, if all the sales and costs which give rise to the £13k operating profit were cash transactions except the depreciation, then the cash flow during the year would be £3k higher than the operating profit. Hence we **add back** depreciation, as shown in Table 4.5.

Impact of trade debtors on cash flow

As it happens, there were other transactions that did not involve cash. £30k worth of sales were made on credit, although, in the course of the year, some of this money was collected. At the end of the year, £15k was still due from customers. The effect of this £15k is that sales that actually became cash in the year were lower than the sales recognised in calculating operating profit. This has the effect of making cash flow lower than operating profit. Thus we subtract £15k from the operating profit.

SILK BLOOMERS LIMITED

Cash flow statement for first year (re-stated)

		£'000
Operating activities		
Operating profit	13.0	
Depreciation	3.0	
Increase in trade debtors	(15.0)	
Increase in stock	(10.0)	
Increase in prepayments	(8.0)	
Increase in trade creditors	12.0	
Increase in accruals	2.0	
		(3.0)
Returns on investments and servicing of finance		
Interest payable on loan		(1.0)
Taxation		
Total		0.0
Capital expenditure		
Purchase of fixed assets		(9.0)
Equity dividends paid		
Total		0.0
Financing		
Shares issued	10.0	
Loan from Sarah's parents	10.0	
		20.0
Net change in cash balance		7.0

Table 4.5 SBL's cash flow statement re-stated

Impact of stock on cash flow

At the end of the year, SBL had some stock it had not sold. This stock was treated as an asset of the company and was not included in the calculation of operating profit for the year. Nonetheless, buying stock requires cash to be spent. The effect of this stock is to make cash flow lower than operating profit. Once again, therefore, we make an adjustment on our cash flow statement.

But that's not necessarily true is it, Chris? Most of the stock was bought on credit and some of it hasn't been paid for yet.

That's a good point, but what we do is to separate the stock from the method of payment. In other words, we assume that the stock was all paid for in cash. If in fact it wasn't, then the balance sheet will show us owing money to the supplier under trade creditors. As you will see in a minute, we adjust the cash flow statement to take account of any trade creditors at the year end.

Impact of prepayments on cash flow

Just as with stock, we have paid out cash which is not included as an expense in our operating profit calculation. Again, this will tend to make cash flow lower than operating profit and we have to make an adjustment downwards.

Impact of trade creditors/accruals on cash flow

Some of the expenses we recognised in calculating our operating profit and some of the stock we have at the year end have not actually been paid for. Our cash flow statement so far assumes that they have, however. We must therefore adjust the cash flow upwards to take account of the creditors and accruals at the year end.

Interpretation of the cash flow statement

Having made these adjustments, the operating activities section of the cash flow statement is now much more useful. We can see at a glance that cash flow (negative £3k) was substantially worse than operating profit (positive £13k) and we can see that this was caused by making sales on credit, building up stock and making a prepayment for some stock. This was offset to some extent by not paying suppliers immediately and by the fact that some of the operating expense was depreciation, which doesn't affect cash.

The effect of a previous year's transactions

I'm looking at Wingate's cash flow statement on page 280, which shows an increase in debtors reducing cash by £370k in year five. According to Wingate's balance sheet on page 279, debtors at the year end were £1,561k. Why aren't these two figures the same?

This is an extremely important point which I was just about to come on to. What you have to remember is that, at the start of the year, most companies will have some debtors left over from the previous year. These debtors will be collected during the current year. Thus you have to allow for the cash you collect from these debtors in your cash flow calculation. The effect of this is that the cash flow adjustment due to debtors is the increase in debtors from the start of the year to the end.

It sounds plausible, Chris, but I don't think I'm really with you. Can you give us an example with numbers?

Of course. Assume you run a company which has been going for a few years. Your sales for this year are £100k and your expenses are £80k, giving you an operating profit of £20k. As we said before, if all your sales and expenses are paid in cash at the time, your cash flow must also be £20k.

Now assume that *last* year some of your customers did *not* pay in cash, so that at the end of that year (i.e. the beginning of this year) you were owed £15k. Those customers paid up during this year so that, on top of receiving the cash from this year's sales, you also received an extra £15k in cash. Your cash flow for the year would be:

	£'000
Operating profit	20
Last year's debtors	15
Total	35

If we now assume that, in fact, some of this year's sales were made on credit and that at the end of the year you are still owed £30k by customers, the cash flow would be £30k lower:

	£'000
Operating profit	20
Last year's debtors	15
This year's debtors	(30)
Total	5

As you can see, what we are actually doing is adjusting operating profit downwards by the increase in debtors (i.e. 30 – 15) between the start and end of the year.

So with SBL it just happened that the debtors at the start of the year were zero, so the increase in debtors was the same as the year end debtors figure, since 15 – 0 = 15?

Exactly. You will notice that I wrote 'Increase in trade debtors' on SBL's cash flow statement. All the other adjustments are identical to this, in that we have to allow for any amounts at the start of the year and thus our adjustments are all based on the increases in the items.

If, for example, trade debtors went down during the year rather than up, what would happen?

Just what the arithmetic would tell you. You would end up getting more cash in than you would have done if all your sales were for cash. Thus your adjustment to operating profit would be upwards rather than downwards.

SUMMARY

- The P&L for a particular period is, at its most simplistic, a list of all the balance sheet entries made during that period which affect retained profit.

- In practice, we summarise these entries and show different 'levels' of profit (gross profit, operating profit, profit before tax, profit after tax).

- The cash flow statement at its most simplistic is a list of all the balance sheet entries for the relevant period which affect cash.

- In practice, we summarise these entries into a number of categories.

- Profit and cash flow from operations are not usually the same during any given period. In the long run, however, they must be the same.

- The usual form of cash flow statement therefore starts with the operating profit for the period and shows why the cash flow during that period was different.

The clever bit is that for any transaction, you must always credit one nominal account and debit another.

5

Book-keeping jargon

- Basic terminology
- The debit and credit convention

We've already seen that double-entry book-keeping isn't half as frightening as it's made out to be. This also applies to 'debits' and 'credits', which you may have heard of. They're nothing more than a convention used to describe double entries. If you are going to have anything at all to do with producing a set of company accounts, this is worth ten minutes of your time.

There are a few other basic terms and concepts that would also be worth knowing about, so I'll start with those and come on to debits and credits shortly.

Basic terminology

Nominal account

Each of the items which makes up the balance sheet is a **nominal account**. So, if we look at SBL's final balance sheet [page 51], we can see that SBL's nominal accounts would be:

Fixed assets	Trade creditors
Stock	Accruals
Prepayments	Tax payable
Trade debtors	Dividends payable
Cash	Share capital
	Retained profit

In practice, accountants like to keep a lot of detail at their finger-tips. They do this by having many more nominal accounts than those listed above.

For example, instead of just one account called fixed assets, they would typically have an account for each different type of fixed asset (e.g. free-hold properties, leasehold properties, plant and equipment, cars, etc.). The sum of all these accounts would add up to the total fixed assets.

Similarly, there would not be one nominal account called retained profit but a separate account for each different type of income and expense that make up retained profit. Thus, SBL would have:

> Sales
> Cost of goods sold
> Car expenses
> Car depreciation
> Equipment rental
> Stationery
> Telephone expenses
> Interest payable
> Tax payable
> Dividend payable

This makes it easy to derive the P&L from the balance sheets as we did in our last session.

A large company may have many hundreds of nominal accounts to help track its revenues and expenses. The principles remain the same of course.

Nominal ledger

All the nominal accounts make up the **nominal ledger**. In the past, the nominal ledger was exactly what its name implies – a large book in which details of each of the nominal accounts were kept. Today the nominal ledger is typically part of a computer program which stores the information about each of the nominal accounts.

Trial balance

The **trial balance** (or 'TB' for short) is just a listing of all the nominal accounts showing the balance in each. In other words, it is just a very detailed balance sheet.

At any time, your accountant can print out the TB and summarise it to give you a balance sheet. Naturally, provided they also have the TB at the start of the month or year, they could then produce the P&L and cash flow statements as well.

Purchase ledger

Most companies have scores of suppliers, if not hundreds or thousands. It is obviously very important to keep detailed records of all transactions with suppliers, so a separate ledger is maintained for this purpose. Again, it is typically part of a computer program today. Such **purchase ledgers** are linked to the nominal ledger so that whenever a change is made to the purchase ledger, the relevant accounts in the nominal ledger (e.g. trade creditors, cash, retained profit) are automatically updated.

Sales ledger

The **sales ledger** is the equivalent of the purchase ledger for customer records. Again, it is typically linked to the nominal ledger so that the relevant nominal accounts are updated.

Posting

When accountants talk about **posting** a transaction, they simply mean they are going to enter it into the relevant ledgers; i.e. into the nominal ledger and the purchase/sales ledgers if applicable.

Audit trail

A listing kept by all accounting systems of every transaction posted onto the system. Even if you reverse (i.e. cancel) a transaction, the audit trail will not delete the erroneous transaction. It will instead record the original transaction and the one made to reverse it.

Journal entry

A journal entry is an adjustment made to the nominal ledger (i.e. to two or more nominal accounts), often an end of period adjustment such as we saw with SBL.

The debit and credit convention

The debit and credit convention is a really neat and simple concept.

Unfortunately, it *appears* to totally contradict something you've taken for granted since you first got a bank account.

Let's start with what you take for granted. If you had £100 on deposit at your bank, you would say you were £100 in credit. If you then paid an extra £50 into your account, your bank would say they had credited your account with £50. Similarly, if you withdrew £50, the bank would say they had debited your account. Hence, we associate crediting with getting bigger or better and debiting with getting smaller or worse. Is that fair?

Perfectly. You're not going to tell us it's wrong?

Not wrong, just not the whole story. What I need you to do now is forget that you associate 'credit' with positive balances and good things and that you associate 'debit' with negative balances and bad things. Can you do that for a few minutes?

If necessary, but the explanation had better be good, Chris.

OK, look at this diagram [Figure 5.1]. This shows a balance sheet chart with the key items (i.e. nominal accounts) that a small to medium-sized company might have. As always, we list all the assets on the left-hand bar and all the claims on the right-hand bar.

Now comes the leap of faith:

- All the nominal accounts on the assets bar are **debit** balances. When you increase one of these boxes, you are **debiting** the account. When you decrease one, you are **crediting** it.

- All the nominal accounts on the claims bar have **credit** balances. When you increase one of these boxes, you are **crediting** the account. When you decrease one, you are **debiting** it.

I'm afraid it's a no-jump, Chris. You're telling me that if I have cash in the bank, that would be a debit balance. You said it yourself: it totally contradicts the banks' conventions.

It doesn't actually. The statements and letters that the bank sends you are looking at your account from the point of view of *their* balance sheet. If you deposit money with your bank, they owe you that money. Thus, from their point of view, your account appears on the claims side of their balance sheet and is thus a credit balance.

On *your* balance sheet, that cash is an asset and is thus a debit balance. Both are consistent with the convention – you just have to be clear whose balance sheet you are talking about.

I think I can see that in principle but I don't see why this convention is so clever or why it helps me.

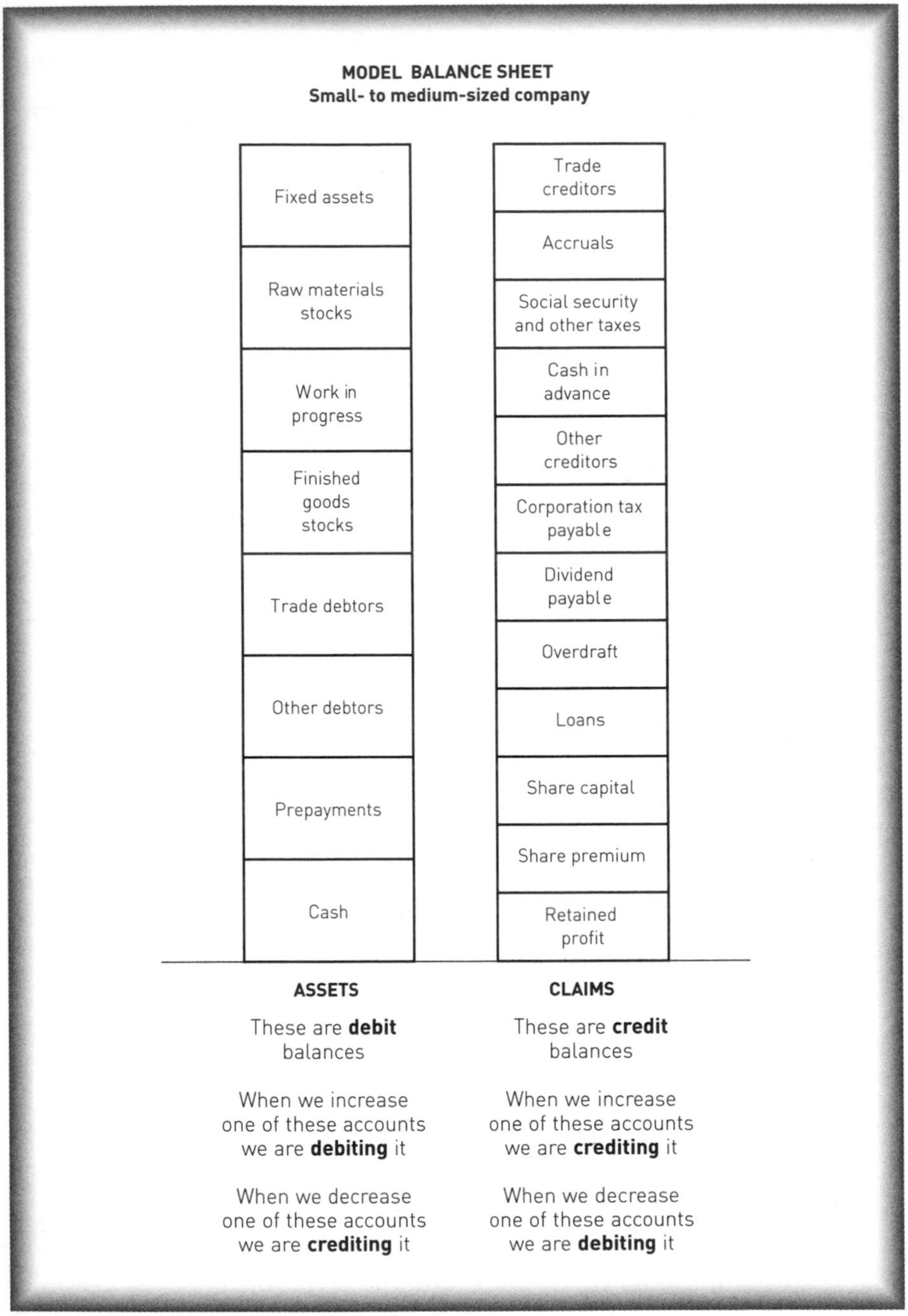

MODEL BALANCE SHEET
Small- to medium-sized company

ASSETS	CLAIMS
Fixed assets	Trade creditors
	Accruals
Raw materials stocks	Social security and other taxes
Work in progress	Cash in advance
	Other creditors
Finished goods stocks	Corporation tax payable
Trade debtors	Dividend payable
	Overdraft
Other debtors	Loans
	Share capital
Prepayments	Share premium
Cash	Retained profit

ASSETS	**CLAIMS**
These are **debit** balances	These are **credit** balances
When we increase one of these accounts we are **debiting** it	When we increase one of these accounts we are **crediting** it
When we decrease one of these accounts we are **crediting** it	When we decrease one of these accounts we are **debiting** it

Figure 5.1 Model balance sheet chart for a small- to medium-sized company

The clever bit is that, for any transaction, you must always credit one nominal account and debit another. This has to be true if you think about it:

- If you *increase* an account on the assets bar, you are debiting the account. To make the balance sheet balance, you must do one of two things. Either you reduce another asset account, which would be crediting that account or you increase an account on the claims bar, which would also be crediting the account. Thus, you have one debit and one credit whatever.

- If you *decrease* an account on the assets bar, you are crediting the account. To make the balance sheet balance, you either increase another asset account, which would be debiting that account, or you decrease an account on the claims bar, which would also be debiting the account. Once again, you have got one credit and one debit.

If we run through some of SBL's transactions, you will see how the convention works in practice.

Let's start with the first transaction we posted for SBL [page 20]. Sarah invested £10,000 cash into SBL in return for shares in the company. This resulted in the cash account going up by £10,000 and the share capital account going up by £10,000.

We would describe this transaction as follows:

Debit cash	£10,000
Credit share capital	£10,000

After this transaction we would say the cash account has a debit balance of £10,000 and the share capital account has a credit balance of £10,000.

Let's now look at transaction three [page 24]. SBL bought a car for £9,000 in cash. The car became a fixed asset of the company. Thus the cash account went down by £9,000 and the fixed assets account went up by £9,000. We would therefore say:

Credit cash	£9,000
Debit fixed assets	£9,000

Transaction nine was paying your car expenses of £4,000. This resulted in cash going down by £4,000 and retained profit going down by £4,000. Thus:

Credit cash	£4,000
Debit retained profit	£4,000

What about something like transaction six where I sold some stock? In that transaction, three nominal accounts changed – stock, cash and retained profit.

That's no problem. What I said earlier about having one debit and one credit wasn't exactly true. You must have at least one debit and at least one credit but you can have more than one of each, *provided that the total debits add up to the total credits for any transaction.* If that weren't the case, the balance sheet wouldn't balance.

In transaction six, we sold £6,000 worth of stock for £12,000 cash Hence, cash went up by £12,000, stock down by £6,000, retained profit up by £6,000. We can thus say:

Debit cash	£12,000
Credit stock	£6,000
Credit retained profit	£6,000

As it happens, accountants take the convention one step further and put the debits in one column and the credits in another as follows:

	Debit	Credit
Cash	12,000	
Stock		6,000
Retained profit		6,000
	———	———
	12,000	12,000

The debits are always in the left-hand column. As you will notice, this is consistent with my balance sheet chart, which has the assets bar on the left.

I think I'm beginning to get the hang of it, and I agree it's quite neat but is it really any use to me?

Maybe, for a couple of reasons.

First, if you have much to do with preparing a company's accounts, there are going to be times when you're unsure of the book-keeping for a particular transaction. More often than not, you'll find that one of the entries is obvious but you are not sure what the other one is. If the

obvious one is, for example, a credit, then you know you are looking for a debit, which usually helps you sort it out in half the time. If you use the convention in conjunction with a balance sheet chart, you'll be way ahead of the game.

Second, you'll find being able to speak their language will not only make it easier but will give you a lot of confidence in dealing with accountants. There's no need to be 'blinded by science' any more.

What I want you to do now is run through all 17 of SBL's transactions and write down the debits and credits that relate to each. Lay them out as I did the last transaction; i.e. with the debits in a column on the left and the credits on the right. Then check your answers against my list [Table 5.1].

Transaction		Debit	Credit
1	**Issue shares**		
	Cash	10,000	
	Share capital		10,000
2	**Loan from parents**		
	Cash	10,000	
	Long-term loans		10,000
3	**Buy car**		
	Cash		9,000
	Fixed assets	9,000	
4	**Buy stock for cash**		
	Cash		8,000
	Stock	8,000	
5	**Buy stock on credit**		
	Stock	20,000	
	Trade creditors		20,000
6	**Sell stock for cash**		
	Cash	12,000	
	Stock		6,000
	Retained profit		6,000

Table 5.1 Debits and credits relating to SBL's transactions

Transaction		Debit	Credit
7	**Sell stock on credit**		
	Stock		12,000
	Trade debtors	30,000	
	Retained profit		18,000
8	**Equipment rental, etc.**		
	Trade creditors		2,000
	Retained profit	2,000	
9	**Car expenses**		
	Cash		4,000
	Retained profit	4,000	
10	**Loan interest**		
	Cash		1,000
	Retained profit	1,000	
11	**Collect cash from debtors**		
	Cash	15,000	
	Trade debtors		15,000
12	**Pay creditors**		
	Cash		10,000
	Trade creditors	10,000	
13	**Prepayment**		
	Cash		8,000
	Prepayments	8,000	
14	**Telephone accrual**		
	Accruals		2,000
	Retained profit	2,000	
15	**Depreciation**		
	Fixed assets		3,000
	Retained profit	3,000	
16	**Accrue tax liability**		
	Tax liability		4,000
	Retained profit	4,000	
17	**Accrue dividend**		
	Dividend liability		3,000
	Retained profit	3,000	

Interpretation of accounts

If you're absolutely clear on everything we've done so far, then you know about 80 per cent of everything you'll ever need to know about accounting.

Wingate's annual report

- Accounting rules
- The reports
- Assets
- Liabilities
- Shareholders' equity
- The P&L and cash flow statement
- The notes to the accounts
- Summary

The first five sessions were devoted to the basics of accounting: the fundamental principle, the balance sheet, double entry, the derivation of the P&L and cash flow statement from the balance sheet. If you're absolutely clear on everything we've done so far, then you know about 80 per cent of everything you'll ever need to know about accounting.

From here on, accounting is just about understanding all the other rules and terminology which have developed over the years. The terminology is fine; the rules can get very complicated, as they have to deal with all sorts of special situations. These special situations are not important at the moment. What you and I need is a broad understanding of the rules. As you will see, there is nothing inherently difficult about any of them.

What we are going to do is work our way through Wingate's annual report and I'll explain anything we haven't already covered in looking at SBL. Just before we do that, though, let me explain where the rules come from and when they have to be applied.

Accounting rules

There are two generic types of 'accounts' you might come across or want to prepare yourself:

- Management accounts
- Statutory accounts

Management accounts are the accounts companies prepare for the use of their directors and management. These accounts, if they are done properly, are based on the fundamental principle of accounting and the two basic concepts we discussed earlier (the accruals basis and the going concern assumption). There are, however, no other requirements as to how they should be laid out, how much detail there should be etc. These things are up to the company to decide. Often, of course, they will obey many of the rules for statutory accounts.

Statutory accounts are the accounts which companies have to file with Companies House each year and make available to their shareholders. There are many rules for such accounts, some of which are set out in the Companies Acts of 1985 and 1989 but most of which are issued by the Accounting Standards Board (the ASB) in the form of Financial Reporting Standards. Despite all the rules, though, there remains considerable scope for very similar companies to choose different accounting policies. The ASB therefore requires that accounting policies should be chosen…

- So as to show a true and fair view of the company's financial position.
- Taking into account:
  - Relevance (of any particular bit of information)
  - Reliability (of the information)
  - Comparability (with similar information from the past or from other companies)

– Understandability (to a reasonably knowledgeable, diligent person)

As we will see later, directors don't always take as much notice of these over-riding requirements as they should.

Let's now look at Wingate's annual report.

The reports

Let's start by looking at the reports, of which there are always at least two.

The directors' report

All companies, other than very small ones, are required by law to provide a directors' report with their annual accounts. The law specifies a number of items that always have to be included in the report, others that have to appear if relevant to the company's situation. Several of these items are just summarising information that appears elsewhere in the accounts, and most of them are self-explanatory anyway, so I won't go through them in detail.

One required item worthy of mention is the listing of directors and their interests in the company. The level of financial involvement directors have in a company can give you an indication of their commitment to the company. Equally, any changes in their levels of holdings can indicate their confidence in the future of the business.

The auditors' report

Most substantial companies have to have their annual accounts **audited**. This just means that a firm of accountants comes in and makes an independent examination of the company's books.

When the accounts are produced for the shareholders (or **members** as they are often called), the auditors have to provide a report, expressing their opinion on the company's financial statements.

The auditors' report usually states simply that:

- They have audited the accounts.

- In their opinion, the accounts give a true and fair view of the company's state of affairs and the changes over the relevant period.

- The accounts have been properly prepared in accordance with the Companies Act 1985.

This is what you would expect, so it doesn't really tell you much. The time to sit up and take notice, however, is when the auditors' report is qualified.

Sometimes, for example, the directors of the company will not agree with the auditors about the way certain items should be accounted for. The directors can insist on taking their approach, rather than the auditors'. In such a case, the auditors would not be happy to make the statements above and they will note the reasons for this in their report. A qualified report is nearly always a bad sign, so watch out for it.

Other reports

Larger companies will often have a **chairman's statement** and/or a **review of operations** and/or a **financial review**. These reports will tell you something about what is going on in the company, but bear in mind that they are usually written by the public relations department and will focus on the positive aspects of the company. Read these reports for what they *don't* say about the company.

Assets

The real substance of the annual report is in the three main financial statements and the notes to those statements

We will now review these in detail. As always, we will start with the balance sheet [page 279], looking first at the assets and then at the claims on those assets. As we go down the balance sheet, we will refer to the relevant notes to make sure we cover everything.

Tangible fixed assets

As you will recall, fixed assets are assets for use in the business on a long-term continuing basis. **Tangible fixed assets** are, as the name implies, fixed assets that you can touch, such as land, buildings, machinery, fixtures and fittings, vehicles, etc.

If you look at the balance sheet on page 279, you can see that there is a single tangible fixed assets figure for each of the two years (£5,326k in year five and £4,445k in year four). This tells us that the tangible assets went up by £881k during the last year.

If you look at Note 9 on page 284, you will see, as I pointed out earlier, that there is a table giving much more detail about the fixed assets.

The first thing to notice about this table is that there are three columns separating the fixed assets into different categories. The three categories are then added together in the fourth column to give the total.

If you look at the bottom right-hand corner of the table, you will see the figures £5,326k and £4,445k. These are the net book value figures which appear on the balance sheets. As I explained earlier, net book value is simply the cost of the assets less the total depreciation on the assets up to that point.

The rest of the table shows how the assets came to have the net book values that they do. To see how this works, we will work our way down the 'Total' column.

Look at the top of the table. The first section, headed 'Cost', shows what the company paid originally for its fixed assets:

- At the start of year five the company had fixed assets which had cost it a total of £6,492k to buy.

- During the year, the company bought fixed assets which cost it another £1,391k.

- Some fixed assets were sold during the year, however. These assets had originally cost £35k. Note that this is not what the company received for the assets when it sold them.

- Thus the original cost of the fixed assets still owned by the company at the end of the year totalled £7,848k (being 6,492 + 1,391 – 35).

The next section shows how the total cumulative depreciation to date was arrived at:

- By the start of year five, the fixed assets of the company had been depreciated by £2,047k. In other words, the company was saying that the fixed assets had been used and were worth less than when they were new.

- Some of that depreciation (£20k), however, related to the fixed assets which the company sold during the year. Since the company no longer owns the assets, we must remove the relevant depreciation from our calculations. Hence, we deduct it from the starting depreciation figure.

- We then have to add the depreciation charge for the year. This is made up of depreciation on the assets which were owned throughout the year plus the depreciation on the assets bought during the year.

- We can then calculate the total depreciation figure for the assets still owned at the end of the year which is £2,522k (being 2,047 – 20 + 495).

Now all we have to do is subtract the depreciation figure from the cost figure to get the net book value figure to go on our balance sheet. Naturally, you can work your way down any one of the three individual fixed asset categories in the table, using the same principles.

Sale of fixed assets

I'm not sure if this is the time to mention it but I'm slightly confused by the sale of some of the fixed assets. I can see how selling an asset will reduce the fixed assets figure on the balance sheet, but what is the other entry?

A good question, but you should be able to work it out for yourself. The note on fixed assets tells us that Wingate sold fixed assets that had an original cost of £35k and total depreciation at the start of the year of £20k. Thus they had a net book value of £15k at the start of the year.

Go back to the balance sheet chart [page 86]. When we sell a fixed asset, the fixed asset box must go down by the net book value of the asset which, in this case, is £15k.

I know from Wingate's accounts (I'll tell you how shortly) that Wingate sold those fixed assets for £23k. Assume that was paid in cash at the time of the sale. Obviously, Wingate's cash box must go up by £23k. The net effect of this and the reduction of the fixed assets box is that Wingate's assets bar goes up by £8k. Something else must change. No other assets or liabilities are affected so it must be the shareholders who benefit. Thus we raise retained profit by £8k. Wingate has made a profit on the sale of the fixed assets of £8k. This profit is declared in Note 3 to the accounts [page 282]

I can see how the accounting works, but it doesn't seem right that we are claiming to have made a profit on selling an asset for £23k when it cost us £35k in the first place.

Your question shows the importance of concentrating on what the balance sheet looks like immediately before and immediately after a transaction. Let's look at what actually happened:

- The assets were bought for £35k.

- Between the date of purchase and the date of sale, the assets were depreciated by £20k. This means that the retained profit of the company was reduced by £20k during that period.

- But, in fact, Wingate sold the assets for £23k. This implies that the total cost to the company of owning the assets for the time it did was only £12k (i.e. 35–23).

- This means that retained profit was reduced by too much in the earlier years. The cost of owning these assets was not as high as £20k – it was only £12k. Hence, when we sell them we have to cancel out the overcharged amount, which we do by showing a profit on sale.

While you've been explaining that to Tom, I've been looking at the effect of this sale on Wingate's cash flow statement. I'm afraid I don't understand it.

Again, we can work it out from first principles. We have just seen that the profit on sale is the difference between what you sell the assets for and their book value in the accounts at the time of sale. Another way of writing this would be:

> Proceeds = Book Value + Profit
> £23k = £15k + £8k

We know that the cash box has gone up by £23k so the cash flow statement must include exactly this amount. Now, if you remember from the cash flow statement we drew up for SBL, we start a cash flow statement with the assumption that cash flow equals operating profit and then adjust it to get to the actual cash flow.

If we start Wingate's cash flow statement with operating profit, then we will automatically have included the profit on sale of the fixed assets (i.e. £8k) because it is included in operating profit (as Note 3 tells us). Thus, to get the total cash flow effect of selling the fixed assets, we just need to make an adjustment to add in the book value of the assets sold. Then both the book value and the profit on sale will be included and we will have accounted for all the proceeds.

In actual fact, we don't do it like this! Instead, we adjust operating profit to remove the £8k profit on sale of the fixed assets. You can see this under the Operating activities section in Wingate's cash flow statement on page 280.

This leaves our cash flow statement without any of the cash proceeds from the sale of the fixed assets. We then include the whole £23k proceeds under the heading 'Capital expenditure'.

The result is the same whichever way you do it. It's all just down to adding and subtracting, as always with accounting. Incidentally, the entry in the cash flow statement is what told me that Wingate had sold those assets for £23k.

Stock

Accounting for stock in SBL's books was straightforward. When Sarah bought stock, we simply increased the stock box by the cost of the stock. When Sarah sold stock, we reduced the stock box by the cost of the stock being sold.

This works fine for many companies, but not for a manufacturer such as Wingate. A manufacturer buys raw materials, makes things with those raw materials and then puts the finished goods into a warehouse, ready to sell to customers. A manufacturer will thus have three types of stock:

- Raw materials
- Work in progress (goods that are partially manufactured at the balance sheet date)
- Finished goods (i.e. goods ready for sale)

Accounting for raw materials is simple. We can treat them in exactly the same way as we did SBL's stock.

What value should we attribute to work in progress and finished goods, though? When we manufacture goods, we take raw materials and do things to them. This involves costs such as rent, electricity, employee wages, depreciation of fixed assets. We call these costs collectively the **production costs**. When we recognise these costs in our accounts, we could 'expense' them as they are incurred. In other words, we would reduce retained profit by the appropriate amounts.

This, however, would be violating the concept of matching. If stock is on the balance sheet, then it has clearly not been sold. Our matching concept says that we should only include expenses that relate to the sales in the relevant year. What we do, therefore, is take the raw materials cost and the associated production costs of any stock that has not been sold and call that the value of the stock. The same principle applies whether we are talking about work in progress or finished goods.

I see that Note 1 (d) [page 282] is about stocks and it says that the costs of production are included in manufactured goods as you have just been saying. What is the rest of this note about, though?

There are two different points here. If some of the stocks are worth less than they cost the company, then, to be conservative, we must decrease their value in the balance sheet (as we say, **write them down**). Thus we say that stock is valued at the lower of cost (where cost would include any costs of production) and **net realisable value** (i.e. what we could sell the stock for).

The other point takes a little more thinking about. Let's go back to SBL, where stock was just bought in rather than manufactured. What would we have done if Sarah had bought two lots of identical stock at different prices, as follows?

- 50 bunches at £20 a bunch (i.e. a total of £1,000)

- 100 bunches at £23 a bunch (i.e. a total of £2,300)

Accounting for the purchase is easy; we simply increase the stock box by £3,300. If Sarah then sold 75 bunches to a customer for £40 a bunch, the sales figure would be £3,000, being 75 × £40. How much would her cost of goods sold be for this transaction, though?

The answer is that it depends! Different companies choose different ways of dealing with this question. Two of the most common ways are the **average** method and **FIFO**.

In the **average** method, we simply take the average cost of stock during the period. In our example this would be:

$$(50 \times £20 + 100 \times £23)/150 = £22 \text{ per bunch}$$

This means that the cost of goods sold for the transaction would be £1,650, being 75 × £22.

FIFO stands for 'First In First Out'. This means that the oldest stock (i.e. that purchased first) is used first. In our example, the oldest stock was purchased for £20. Unfortunately, we only have 50 bunches of that stock, so we then 'use' some of the next oldest stock. Our cost of goods sold is therefore:

$$50 \times £20 + 25 \times £23 = £1,575$$

You've got the same sales in each case, but different cost of goods sold. That means you're going to get different profit figures, doesn't it?

Yes, it does. When we talked about accounting rules earlier, I said that two very similar companies could have different accounts. This is one of the reasons. The key point to remember is that the 'comparability' rule means that companies should use the same method every year. The method they use will be disclosed in the accounting policies in the annual report, as you can see it has been for Wingate.

Trade debtors and doubtful debts

Accounting for debtors is simple. We saw how to do it when we looked at SBL. The only thing you have to consider is the effect of bad debts or doubtful debts. If:

- you know that one of your customers has gone bust owing you money which they will not be able to pay, or
- you think that one of your customers is likely to go bust and not be able to pay you, or
- you have lots of customers and you know that on average a certain percentage of what you are owed will never be paid

then you should make an allowance for those non-payments. If you know for certain that you will not get paid, then you **write off** the debt. If you only think you might not get paid, then you make a **provision** against the debt.

Whether you are writing off a debt or just making a provision, the accounting is the same:

- *Decrease* Debtors.
- *Decrease* Retained profit.

What if you make a provision against a debt that you think may not be paid, but subsequently it is?

You have to reverse the transaction. Effectively, it will show up as an additional profit in your next set of accounts:

- *Increase* Cash.

- *Increase* Retained profit.

Prepayments/other debtors

Again, the accounting treatment is identical to that which we used when constructing SBL's balance sheet.

Cash

As I explained when we were putting SBL's accounts together, the term 'cash' to a company has a different meaning from that used by individuals. An individual thinks of cash as being coins and notes, as opposed to cheques, credit cards or money at the bank.

To a company, cash means money which it can get its hands on quickly in order to pay people. Thus money in a current account would qualify as cash. In fact, even money tied up in a deposit account for several months usually counts as cash.

Liabilities

We have now looked at all the assets on Wingate's balance sheet. I hope you agree that there is nothing very difficult about the accounting there, as long as we stick by our fundamental principle. Now we need to look at the various liabilities.

Trade creditors

There is no difficulty here. The accounting is just the same as for SBL.

Social security and other taxes

Companies with employees have to pay the National Insurance and Income Tax on the wages and salaries which they pay those employees. These charges are normally paid two to three weeks after the end of each month, so they usually show up as a liability on any balance sheet which is drawn up at the end of a month.

Value added tax (VAT) payable to Customs and Excise is also normally included under this category. VAT is a whole subject on its own ...

Value added tax (VAT)

Before you go into VAT, can you tell me what 'value added' is?

A company buys in raw materials, equipment, services; these are the company's **inputs**. The company's employees then do things to or with these inputs in order to make products or provide services. The products and/or services are then sold; these are the company's **outputs**. **Value added** is the difference between the outputs and the inputs; in other words, it's the amount of value that the employees add to the inputs.

So what is VAT?

VAT is exactly what it says: a tax on the value added in products and services. The rules can be very complex but, in general terms, it works as follows.

Most products and services are subject to VAT, although some are classified as **exempt** or **zero-rated**, in which case VAT is not charged. Companies fall into one of two groups as far as VAT is concerned: those which are **VAT registered** and those which aren't. You register for VAT if your annual sales are more than a certain figure (the figure changes every year, but it is of the order of £50,000). If you are registered, you

have to charge VAT on the products you sell (your outputs) and then pass the VAT on to Customs & Excise. You can, however, reclaim from Customs & Excise the VAT you pay on most of the products you buy (your inputs). Thus a company that is registered for VAT does not actually pay any VAT, it merely collects it for Customs and Excise.

So who does pay the tax?

You, me and the other 50 million people in the country. We are charged VAT by the shops when we buy things. Since we are not VAT registered, we cannot reclaim the VAT.

So how does this affect Wingate's accounts?

Let's look at a simple example. The rate of VAT is changed every once in a while (and can be different rates on different categories of products or services), but we will assume it is 15 per cent. If Wingate sells some stock for £1,000, it has to add 15 per cent VAT to that, making a total charge to the customer of £1,150. If Wingate's cost of goods sold was £700, then the accounting entries would be as in Table 6.1.

Assets bar	
Reduce stock	(700)
Increase debtors	1,150
Increase in assets	450
Claims bar	
Increase VAT liability	150
Increase retained profit	300
Increase in liabilities	450

Table 6.1 Accounting for VAT

As you can see, the VAT does not affect retained profit at all. The customer is charged the VAT, but we immediately increase the liability to Customs & Excise by the same amount.

When you make purchases, you will be charged VAT. The VAT element of each purchase *reduces* your liability to Customs & Excise and does not affect retained profit.

Every three months, the balance in the 'VAT liability' box is either paid to Customs & Excise or reclaimed from them, depending on whether the balance is positive or negative. A profitable firm will normally have higher outputs than inputs and thus will owe Customs & Excise.

The last point to make is that, while the sales figure which appears on a company's P&L won't include VAT, the debtors figure on the balance sheet will. We have to remember this when we come to analyse the accounts later.

Accruals

Accruals are exactly as I described them when we were drawing up SBL's balance sheet. They are any costs that need to be included in the accounts to satisfy our matching concept, but where no invoice has been received. Unlike the trade creditors figure, accruals will not normally include VAT.

Cash in advance (Deferred revenue/income)

There are many companies that can justify charging their customers in advance of delivering the goods. Often this is just a deposit; in other cases it might be full payment for something, such as a subscription to a magazine.

Whatever the situation, when a company receives cash in advance, it cannot recognise that cash as revenue until the goods or services have been provided to the customer. Until then, the company has a liability

to the customer. Referring to the balance sheet chart again [page 86], we account for cash in advance as follows:

- *Increase* Cash.

- *Increase* Cash in advance.

Be clear that cash in advance is not cash. It is a liability you have to customers who have given you cash upfront. A better term might be 'owed to customers'.

So what happens when you deliver the goods?

Simple – you can now recognise the profit on the sale:

- *Decrease* Stock.

- *Decrease* Cash in advance.

- *Increase* Retained profit.

This removes the liability to the customer and increases the wealth of the shareholders. This is in accordance with our accounting principles as the goods have now been delivered.

Bank overdraft

Most of us are all too familiar with overdrafts. They are simply current accounts with a negative amount of cash in them. Many companies have such accounts from which they pay all their day-to-day bills and into which they put the cash they receive from customers.

As they do with individuals, banks usually grant an **overdraft facility** to companies. This means that the company can run up an overdraft to a specified limit. There is not normally any time limit on overdraft facilities, but the banks nearly always retain the right to demand immediate repayment. This is why they are treated as current rather than long-term liabilities.

Taxation

In principle, **corporation tax** is very simple. A company makes sales and incurs expenses to do so. After paying interest on any loans, overdrafts, etc. the company makes a profit (profit before tax) which is 'due' to the shareholders. The Inland Revenue takes a share of that profit by taxing it. This is corporation tax. Large companies have to pay corporation tax in instalments during their financial year, while small companies pay it nine months after the end of the company's financial year. Thus a small company's balance sheet usually shows a corporation tax liability under current liabilities.

This straightforward situation is made complicated because corporation tax is actually calculated as a percentage of **taxable income** rather than profit before tax. Taxable income is different from profit before tax for all sorts of reasons and often requires complex calculations. For example, if a company has made losses in previous years, those losses can be carried forwards to reduce taxable income in the current year. The Inland Revenue also has its own way of allowing for depreciation (called capital allowances) so this will create a difference between taxable income and profit before tax in almost all companies. The ASB now requires companies to give a summary of how taxable income differs from profit before tax. The percentage of taxable income payable as tax varies depending on the size of the company, though most medium and large companies will pay at the highest rate which changes from year to year but is around 30 per cent.

Dividends

A company can pay a dividend to its shareholders as often as it likes, subject to a legal restriction. The legal restriction is, broadly speaking, that a company's retained profit must always be greater than zero. Thus, if paying a dividend would take the retained profit below zero, the company cannot legally pay the dividend.

In practice, most companies pay dividends once or twice a year. Often they will declare an **interim dividend** half-way through their financial year and a **final dividend** at the end of the year. The dividends are usually paid three to six months after being declared. Final dividends have to be approved by the shareholders at the annual general meeting of the company, which is why Wingate's accounts describe the dividend as 'proposed'.

Some very large companies, and particularly American companies, pay dividends four times a year.

Bank loans

Bank loans are very similar to personal loans. They are made to enable specific purchases of equipment, buildings and other assets to be made. Terms for repayment of the **principal** (i.e. the amount of the loan) and interest payments are agreed in advance. The loan agreement may have other conditions and restrictions which are known as **covenants**. Provided the borrower does not breach the covenants, the bank usually does *not* have the right to demand immediate repayment.

A bank loan is nearly always accompanied by a **charge** or **lien** over the assets of the company. A charge guarantees the bank that, if the company gets into financial difficulty, the bank can have first claim to the proceeds from selling assets which are included in the charge. If the bank has a charge over a specific asset, the charge is known as a **fixed charge** or **mortgage**. This is identical to the charge that the building society has over your house. If the bank's charge is over other assets of the company, such as stock or debtors, where the actual, specific assets change from day to day as the company trades, it is known as a **floating charge**.

Shareholders' equity

Share capital

There are various types of share capital that a company can have. Wingate only has **ordinary shares**, which are by far the most common type. Ordinary shares usually entitle the holder to a proportionate share of the dividends and to vote at meetings of the shareholders. If the company is wound up (i.e. it stops trading) and there are any excess proceeds after paying off the liabilities, then the ordinary shareholders share them out in proportion to the number of shares they hold.

The shareholders of a company agree the maximum number of shares the company should be allowed to issue. This is the **authorised** number. When investors pay money into the company, shares are **allotted** to them (i.e. shares are **'issued'**). Ordinary shares all have a **par** or **nominal** value. This is the lowest value at which the shares can be allotted. Although it is usual, it is not necessary for the full price of a share to be paid into the company when the share is allotted. If any shares are not **fully paid**, however, there is still a legal obligation on the investor to pay the rest on demand by the directors of the company, even if the investor might prefer not to!

If you look at Note 14 on page 285, you can see that 1,500,000 shares of 5p par value have been authorised, but only 1,000,000 have actually been allotted. Those that have been allotted have been fully paid up.

Share premium

I mentioned just now that shares cannot be allotted for less than the par value. They can be, and frequently are, allotted for more than par value. The amount over and above par value that is paid for a share is called the **share premium**. This is recorded separately on the balance sheet.

We can see that Wingate has allotted shares with a total premium of £275k. The *total* capital put into the company by the shareholders is the

sum of the called up share capital and the **share premium**. In Wingate's case this is £50k plus £275k, making total capital invested of £325k.

Retained profit

Hopefully, by now, the meaning of retained profit is reasonably clear. To recap, it's the total profit that the company has made throughout its existence that has not been paid out to shareholders as dividends.

Let me emphasise again that retained profit is *not* the amount of cash the company has. Retained profit is usually made up of all sorts of different assets.

The P&L and cash flow statement

As far as the P&L and cash flow statement are concerned, we covered most of the points when looking at SBL. There are a few things I should mention, however.

Continuing operations

If Wingate had either made an acquisition of another business during the year or had discontinued one or more parts of its operations during the year, the P&L would show them broken out separately so you could see the figures for the continuing operations of the company. This can make a P&L look more complicated but it is actually giving you useful information.

Extraordinary items

Occasionally, an event will occur that causes a company to earn some income or incur some expense which it would not expect in the ordinary course of its business and which it does not expect to recur, i.e. it is a 'one-off' event. The income or expense resulting from this event is called an extraordinary item.

As the P&L shows, Wingate incurred an extraordinary expense of £6,000 during year five. As Note 7 on page 283 explains, this was due to the unrecovered portion of a ransom payment. Clearly, this falls outside the ordinary activities of the company and hopefully will not recur!

Exceptional items

Occasionally, an event will occur in the course of the ordinary activities of a company that gives rise to an income or expense that has a significant impact on the accounts. Such items have to be disclosed separately under the heading exceptional items.

Wingate had no exceptional items in either of years four or five. To give you an example, however, if the profit on the sale of the fixed assets had been larger, this would have been disclosed as an exceptional item.

Earnings per share

As we will see when we get around to talking about the valuation of companies, many investors and analysts use a measure called earnings per share (or eps) to make their valuations. 'Earnings' is another word for 'profit for the year'. If you are a small investor in a company, you know how much you paid for each share and it is often helpful to know how much profit the company made for each of those shares. This figure is shown as the last line on the P&L.

We would calculate earnings per share for Wingate in year five as follows:

Earnings per share = **Profit for year / Number of shares**

= £422k / 1m

= 42.2 pence per share

If Wingate had issued new shares *during the year*, we would use the weighted average number of shares in issue during the year. This means the average number of shares in issue, adjusted for how much of the year they had been in issue.

Cash flow statement detail

The cash flow statement we produced for SBL, while providing the information we required, did not contain everything a modern cash flow statement has to provide.

In addition to the six headings we used for SBL's cash flow statement and which we can see on Wingate's statement [page 280], there are three other headings you will see on some companies' accounts depending on their circumstances

- **Dividends from joint ventures and associates** which is pretty much self-explanatory

- **Acquisitions and disposals** which includes cash in or out in relation to the acquisition and disposal of a business or an investment in a joint venture, subsidiary company etc.

- **Management of liquid resources** which shows when companies have moved cash in or out of short-term deposit accounts or similar investments which are not counted as being 'cash' for the purposes of showing the company's cash flow.

Does this mean that, if the company did nothing in a year other than move some cash out of its current account into a 90-day notice deposit account, the cash flow statement would show an outflow of cash?

Yes, that is exactly what it means, because you can't spend that cash in the 90-day account today (at least not without paying a penalty). This shouldn't bother you, though, because you can see these amounts on the cash flow statement, so if you wanted to call them all cash, you could adjust the cash flow statement yourself.

If you look at Wingate's cash flow statement [pages 280–281], you will see that there are two analyses at the end which we did not produce for SBL. These provide a little more information about the net debt of the company. Net debt is the total debt (overdrafts, loans etc.) less the cash the company has. Usually, you can deduce these analyses yourself from the main statements and the notes but it's always nice to have someone do the work for you.

The notes to the accounts

We have already covered most of the notes to the accounts that are not self-explanatory.

We have not, however, discussed Note 1(a) [page 282]. This note says that the accounts were prepared under the **historical cost convention**. What does this mean?

All the entries on our balance sheets to date have been based on the actual cost of something, i.e. the historic cost. In times of very high inflation, these figures can become meaningless. There is thus an argument for using **current cost**, i.e. the cost of the assets today. Very few companies which you are likely to come across use current cost accounting, so it is not worth spending any time on it now. You should always be clear, though, which convention applies.

Terminology

As you may have discovered already, there are a lot of different terms for the same thing in the accounting world. Even more confusingly, some terms mean different things to different people.

I started out in our first couple of sessions using terminology that I felt best described what we were talking about. In discussing Wingate, I have tried to stick with the same terminology as far as possible.

The 1985 Companies Act actually lays down various terms which must be used in official company accounts. I have avoided some of these terms because I think they are confusing initially. Knowing what you do now, you will have no trouble relating the terms you see in other company accounts to those I have been using here. There is one term, however, that I should explain briefly.

I have been using the term **shareholders' equity** to mean the share of the assets 'due' to the shareholders. In Wingate's case, this is made up of share capital, share premium and retained profit.

The official term is **capital and reserves**. I don't like the word 'reserves' as it sounds too much like cash put away for a rainy day and, as we all know by now, shareholders' equity is not just cash, is it!

While we're on the subject, you will often see 'shareholders' equity' referred to as **shareholders' funds**. I don't like this description either, because the word 'funds' also suggests cash.

That completes our look at Wingate's accounts. Before we look at some other features of accounts you might come across, let me just repeat the crucial points.

SUMMARY

- The fundamental principle of accounting is extremely simple.
- *All* company accounts are based on this principle, but appear more complicated due to the rules and associated terminology needed to accommodate modern business practices.
- Provided you apply the fundamental principle, and always consider the effect of any particular transaction on the balance sheet first, the rules and terminology will give you no difficulty.

I do not propose to go into the accounting in detail, but merely to explain the principles of the relevant accounting rules.

7

Further features of company accounts

- Investments
- Associates and subsidiaries
- Accounting for associates
- Accounting for subsidiaries
- Funding
- Debt
- Equity
- Revaluation reserves
- Statement of recognised gains and losses
- Note of historical cost profits and losses
- Intangible fixed assets
- Leases
- Corporation tax
- Exchange gains and losses
- Fully diluted earnings per share
- Summary

In our review of Wingate's accounts we have covered the majority of the things you will see in the accounts of a small- to medium-sized company.

However, most of the companies in which you might want to invest your spare cash, Tom, are rather larger than Wingate. These companies tend to have somewhat more complex accounts. In fact, at first glance, their accounts can be quite daunting. Don't be intimidated! In the next couple of hours, we can get a good enough understanding of the main features that cause these complexities for you to be able to read such

accounts with considerable confidence. I do not propose to go into the accounting in detail, but merely to explain the principles of the relevant accounting rules.

Investments

One of the first things you will notice about many larger companies' annual reports is that the main statements are described as 'consolidated'. To understand this, we need to discuss investments and how we account for them.

What are investments?

Broadly speaking, an asset that is not used directly in the operation of a company's business is classified as an investment. This definition would include, for example:

- Antique furniture or paintings held in the hope of a rise in value, rather than simply for use in the business.
- Shares in other companies bought as an alternative to putting some spare cash in the bank.
- Shares in other companies bought for strategic reasons, i.e. they form part of the company's long-term strategy. Such investments are known as **trade investments**. Many companies own 100 per cent of the shares of other companies, but trade investments can be of much smaller shareholdings as well.

Companies whose shares can be bought and sold through a recognised stock exchange are described as **listed**. Company accounts have to distinguish between **listed investments** and **unlisted investments**.

Are investments current or fixed assets?

That depends on the type of investment. If you expect to sell the investment in the coming year, then you classify it as a current asset. Otherwise, it is a fixed asset.

Accounting for investments

All investments, regardless of the type, are included on the balance sheet at the lower of the following:

- The cost of the investment,
- The **market value** of the investment, i.e. what you would get if you were to sell the investment.

There is a difference, however, between fixed asset investments and current asset investments. In the case of fixed assets, we only reduce the value on the balance sheet if there has been a permanent diminution in value of the investment. In the case of current assets, we apply the rule at each balance sheet date.

So if I buy some shares on the stockmarket and they triple in value, I would still record them on the balance sheet at what I paid for them, but if they go down in value, I would have to include them at the lower value?

I'm afraid so.

That doesn't seem very sensible – what's the logic behind it?

The logic is simply that you shouldn't include a gain in your accounts until you have **realised** the gain; in other words, until you have sold the investment. This is because the investment's value may go back down again before you sell the shares. Similarly, if the investment's value falls, we pessimistically assume it is not going to go up again.

The rules are different for companies whose business is investing in shares.

Associates and subsidiaries

As you just pointed out, Tom, the way we account for investments means that, if the investment does well, we don't show the benefit of that in the accounts of the investor company.

Many companies, however, carry on a large percentage of their business through investments in other companies. This may be because they have bought the companies (in total or just substantial stakes in them) or because they have started new businesses through separate companies. The way we account for investments means that you wouldn't get a very meaningful picture of such an investor company.

We therefore define certain investments as either **associated undertakings** or **subsidiary undertakings**. They are usually just known as **associates** and **subsidiaries** and there are special rules by which we account for them.

So how are associates and subsidiaries defined?

The rules are actually quite complex, but very generally:

- A company is a subsidiary of yours if you own more than 50 per cent of the voting rights or you are able to exert a dominant influence over the running of that company.

- A company is usually an associate of yours if it is not a subsidiary, but you own 20 per cent or more of the voting rights.

However, if you own less than 20 per cent but still exert a significant influence over the company's affairs, then it is an associate. Similarly, if you own more than 20 per cent but *don't* exert a significant influence, it is not an associate.

Let's now look at how we account for each of these in turn.

Accounting for associates

Accounting for associates is very simple, in principle. The investor company, rather than putting just the cost of the investment on its balance sheet, instead recognises its share of the net assets of the associate. By 'its share' I mean the percentage of the associate's share capital that the investor company owns. This is known as the **equity method**.

So if, during a year, the associate makes a profit (thereby increasing its net assets), the investor company would make the following double entry on its balance sheets:

- *Increase* Share of net assets of associate.

- *Increase* Retained profit.

Since the investor company's retained profit has gone up, its P&L must naturally reflect this. In fact, the investor's P&L shows its share of the associate's profit before tax, tax charge, extraordinary items and retained profit.

So not only is the performance of the associate reflected in the investor company's accounts, but you are actually given some details about that performance. This information is not sufficient to enable you to analyse the associate properly, however; for that you need a copy of the associate's own annual report.

Goodwill

Up to now, we have been learning about accounting on the basis that the net assets of a company (which are equal to the shareholders' equity) represent the value of the shares to the shareholders. Thus, if an investor company was going to buy 20 per cent of a company, we would expect it to pay 20 per cent of the net asset value of the company.

For all sorts of reasons, investors (both companies and individuals) often pay more than net asset value for shares in companies. We will go

into why they do this later. For now, we can think of companies as having various assets that are not included on their balance sheets. Such assets might include:

- An organisation of skilled employees with procedures, culture, experience, etc.

- Relationships with customers and suppliers

- Brand names

These 'hidden' assets lead investors to pay more than net asset value. The difference between what an investor company pays and net asset value is known as **goodwill**. Think of it as representing the goodwill of the associate's customers and suppliers towards the company.

Accounting for goodwill

So is the goodwill shown on the balance sheet?

Yes. So if a company invests, say, £12m to buy 25 per cent of a company which has total net assets at the time of £20m, then the investor company would have less cash assets by £12m but higher 'share of net assets of associates' by £5m (being 25 per cent of £20m) and higher goodwill by £7m (being the £12m cash invested less the £5m that is represented by the actual recorded net assets of the associate).

So in the jargon, we are

- *Crediting cash* £12m
- *Debiting share of net assets of associates* £5m
- *Debiting goodwill* £7m

Yes. There is a further twist on this, however. The investor company is required to treat the goodwill like any other fixed asset and depreciate it over its useful life. This is usually called **amortisation** rather than depreciation but it is the same thing. So if the investor company decides the useful life of the investment is 15 years, it would have to reduce the value of the goodwill by £467k each year for 15 years. The double entry for this is, inevitably, retained profit, so the investor company has a cost of £467k in its P&L every year for 15 years as a result of making this investment.

How do you decide what the useful life of an investment in an associate is?

With difficulty. Many investor companies would argue that the useful life is infinite and that there should therefore be no annual goodwill amortisation. This is allowed under the rules but the investor company has to subject the investment to an 'annual impairment review'. In fact, this applies to all investments a company has where the goodwill amortisation period is greater than 20 years. If the annual impairment review shows the value of the investment to be lower than the value in the investor company's balance sheet, the investor company has to write-down the investment (i.e. reduce the value of the goodwill in its balance sheet and reduce retained profit accordingly).

Accounting for subsidiaries

In principle, accounting for subsidiaries is even easier than accounting for associates. The objective is simply to present the accounts as if the investor company (usually known as the 'parent') and the subsidiaries were all actually part of the same company. This gives you the **consolidated** accounts, which make it very easy for someone interested in the company to get the full picture.

In practice, 'doing consolidations' is not as easy as my description suggests. Since you're never likely to want to do one, it doesn't matter. To interpret a set of consolidated accounts, there are just a few additional things you need to know.

Company vs consolidated balance sheets

Any company which produces consolidated accounts produces a consolidated version of each of the three main financial statements. In addition, the company's unconsolidated balance sheet will also be provided. Generally, this will not be of much interest to you. The consolidated statements are what you should concentrate on.

Goodwill

As with associates, goodwill rears its ugly head where subsidiaries are concerned. The same accounting policies apply.

There is an additional complication. On making acquisitions of subsidiaries, companies have to include the assets of the new subsidiary on their balance sheet at the 'fair value', which is often different from the value in the books of the subsidiary. The goodwill is then the difference between what the investor company paid for the subsidiary and the fair value of the subsidiary's assets.

Minority interests

When an investor company owns less than 100 per cent of a subsidiary, it still consolidates the accounts as if it owned 100 per cent. The investor's accounts are then adjusted to take account of the proportion it does not own. This proportion is known as the **'minority interests'**. You will find 'minority interests' adjustments on all three main consolidated statements.

Funding

When SBL started up, it obtained its funding (or **capital**, as it is often known) from two sources – Sarah and her parents. The cash Sarah put in was ordinary share capital. It was a long-term investment which could only pay a dividend if the company did well. The better the company did, the better would be Sarah's **return** (i.e. the profit on her investment). This form of funding we call **equity** or **share** capital.

The cash Sarah's parents put in was a loan. This was different from Sarah's investment in that the length of the loan (the **term**) was known and the return (the **interest rate**) on the loan was not only known but *had* to be paid, unlike dividends on share capital. This kind of capital is known as **debt**.

There are many different forms of both equity and debt, often called **instruments**, and it can actually be difficult sometimes to tell one from the other. I will run through some of the more common types you are likely to encounter.

Debt

Wingate had two types of debt – an overdraft and a loan. Both of these were provided by the bank. Most of the debt of small- and medium-sized companies is provided in one of these two forms by banks.

Larger companies, however, often 'issue' debt to individual investors or big institutions such as pension funds or insurance companies. This means that the investor provides cash to the company in return for a certificate saying that the company will pay a certain interest rate on the loan and will repay the loan on a certain date. There are often other conditions attached. This kind of debt has many different descriptions, the most common being **loanstock, notes,** or **bonds**. Don't worry about the word used, they are all essentially the same; it is the particular conditions of the debt that are important.

Usually these types of debt can be traded; in other words, once the company has issued the debt, investors can buy and sell the certificates from one another, just as they would buy and sell shares.

Let's look at some examples of different types of debt.

Unsecured loanstock

As we saw when we looked at Wingate's accounts, many loans are secured by a charge. This means that, in the event that the company is unable to pay the interest on the loan or to make the agreed repayments of principal, the lender has the first claim on any proceeds from selling assets which are charged.

Unsecured loanstock is a loan which has no such security. If the company goes bust, then the holders of the unsecured loanstock will have the same rights to any proceeds as the other ordinary creditors of the company. Investors typically require a higher rate of interest on such debt to compensate them for the higher risk they are taking.

Subordinated loanstock

Some loans are **subordinated** to the other creditors of the company. This means that, in the event of a liquidation of the company's assets, the subordinated lenders do not get anything until the other creditors of the company have been paid in full. Such loans are therefore even more risky than unsecured loans and carry a higher interest rate.

Debentures

These are loans which carry a fixed rate of interest for a fixed term. Usually, they are secured on the company's assets.

Fixed rate notes

A fixed rate note is exactly what it says: a loan at a fixed rate of interest. Usually, it will have a specified date on which it will be repaid.

Floating rate notes

A floating rate note is a loan which has an interest rate linked to one of the interest rate standards – such as the Base Rate, which is the rate set by the Bank of England, or LIBOR, which is the short-term rate of interest on loans between banks.

Convertible bonds

These are loans which permit the lenders to convert the bonds into ordinary shares in the company instead of being repaid the principal. The bond pays interest until conversion takes place. The price and dates at which conversion can take place are specified in advance. These bonds pay a lower rate of interest than an ordinary bond, which is what makes them attractive to the issuing company.

Zero coupon bonds

Coupon is just another word for interest. This is a loan which pays no interest! Instead, it pays the lender a lump sum at the end of the term which is greater than the original loan amount. Thus the bond is effectively paying interest; you just don't get it until the end of the term.

How do you account for a zero coupon bond, then? Is the liability the initial amount or the final amount?

The liability starts as the amount of cash received for the bond, but the liability increases each year. As I said, interest is effectively paid on this type of loan, and we can work out what the effective interest rate is. We then increase the liability by this interest rate each year so that, at the end of the term, the liability has grown to the final lump sum payment. The other book-keeping entry is to reduce retained profit each year by the effective interest for the year.

Equity

As we saw in the last session, Wingate has only one type (or **class** as it is known) of share capital – ordinary shares. These are by far the most

common shares you will encounter. Just as with debt, though, there are variations.

Preference shares

The shares you are likely to encounter most often after ordinary shares are **preference shares**. They are different from ordinary shares in that:

- They usually have a fixed annual dividend, which must be paid before any dividend is paid on the ordinary shares. Unlike interest, though, these dividends cannot be paid unless the company has positive retained profit.

- If the company is wound up, the preference shareholders usually get their money back before any money is returned to the ordinary shareholders. The amount they get back will, however, be the amount they put in or some other predetermined amount. The ordinary shareholders get what is left over, which may be a lot more than they put in or a lot less.

The result of this is that preference shares are less risky than ordinary shares because they come before the ordinary shares in everything (hence the name preference), but there is less opportunity for the preference shares to become worth a huge amount.

There are many variations on simple preference shares. For example:

- Sometimes a company may not be performing very well and may not be able to pay a dividend in a particular year. **Cumulative** preference shares entitle the holders to get all their dividends due from past years, as well as the current year's, before any dividends can be paid to ordinary shareholders.

- Sometimes preference shares include conditions whereby the dividend on the shares will be increased (i.e. when the company does particularly well). These are known as **participating** preference shares.

- Some preference shares have a fixed date on which the company must return the capital invested by the preference shareholders. These are known as **redeemable** preference shares.

- Some preference shares can be converted into ordinary shares at a certain time and certain price per ordinary share. These are known as **convertible** preference shares.

As you can see, preference shares can actually be a lot of very different things! Indeed, they can be all of these things at once, which gives you this:

*Cumulative participating redeemable convertible
preference shares*

Other types of shares

A company can issue shares with more or less any terms and conditions it chooses (provided the shareholders agree) and these shares can be called whatever the company chooses. There are two types of share which are fairly common:

- Some companies issue shares which are identical to ordinary shares except that they have no rights to vote at meetings of ordinary shareholders. Such shares are typically used by family companies which want to issue shares to new investors so that they can raise some additional funds, but where the family does not want to lose control of the company. Using these shares, the family can retain more than 50 per cent of the voting rights, while not necessarily keeping more than 50 per cent of the financial benefits of the share capital.

  These shares are usually called **A shares** but they can be called anything. Equally, shares with completely different terms and conditions could be called 'A Shares'.

- **Deferred shares** are more or less the opposite of the shares I've just described. They usually have voting rights, but no rights to dividends

until the profits of the company reach a certain level. Other criteria may apply as well.

Options

Employees of companies are often given options over ordinary shares. These options give the employee the right, within certain time periods, to make the company issue them with shares at a predetermined price (known as the **exercise price**). If the share price of a company goes above the exercise price, then the option-holder can 'exercise' the option, pay the exercise price to the company and then sell the shares for an instant profit.

These options are used as an incentive to the employees to raise the share price of the company.

Revaluation reserves

To date, I have repeated several times that accountants always take the conservative viewpoint. The result of this is that if an asset, such as stock, falls in value, we would 'write it down'. On the other hand, if the value of an asset rises, we would not write it up.

There is a common exception to this rule: land and buildings.

Unlike most other fixed assets, land and buildings have tended to in-crease in value over time. Accounting standards permit this value to be included in the accounts. The effect of a revaluation is to increase the shareholders' wealth. You might therefore assume that to account for this, we would increase fixed assets and increase retained profit.

We do, indeed, increase fixed assets but, instead of adjusting retained profit, we create a **revaluation reserve**. Revaluation reserves are part of shareholders' equity so a revaluation of land and buildings does show up as an increase in the shareholders' wealth. The reason for excluding revaluations from retained profit is that the increase in value of the assets has not yet been realised. It remains a hypothetical increase until the assets are actually sold. As I mentioned earlier, a company cannot pay dividends unless its retained profits are greater than zero. Thus the rule ensures that revaluation 'profits' are not paid out to shareholders as dividends before they are actually realised.

Statement of recognised gains and losses

Where a company has recognised an unrealised gain or loss (like revaluation) – i.e. where the gain or loss has not been included in retained profit and therefore does not show up in the P&L – the company has to include an additional statement called the 'statement of recognised gains and losses'. This statement does not actually provide any additional information but simply summarises all the gains and losses for the year, whether realised or not. As well as revaluations of assets, other items you will encounter in this statement include gains or losses on currency translation and prior year adjustments.

If, as in Wingate's case, there are no recognised gains or losses other than those shown in the P&L, a statement to that effect is usually made at the bottom of the P&L (see page 278).

Note of historical cost profits and losses

Where a company has revalued an asset in a previous year and then sold it in the current year, the accounting gets a little curious (to me, at least). Suppose you bought a building some time ago for £6m. *Last* year, you had it valued and concluded it was worth £9m. You therefore followed the accounting rules we've just been talking about: increase fixed assets on the assets bar by £3m and create a revaluation reserve of £3m on the claims bar; produce a statement of recognised gains and

losses showing this additional £3m of gain that does not show up in the P&L.

Assume now that in the *current* financial year, you actually sell the building for £11m. You would hope that you could show the full £5m profit in your P&L – since this is the profit you have made since buying the building. This would be easy in accounting terms:

- Increase cash by £11m, reduce fixed assets by £9m – thereby increasing the assets bar by a net £2m
- Increase retained profit by £5m, lower revaluation reserve by £3m – thereby increasing the claims bar by a net £2m.

You would then show the £5m increase in retained profit in your P&L. In fact, while you do make the accounting entries I describe, you aren't allowed to include the full £5m profit in your P&L. You are only allowed to show £2m, being the difference between the sale price (£11m) and revalued amount in your books (£9m). The other £3m of profit you show in a summary statement called the 'Note of historical cost profits and losses'.

So in this scenario, your retained profit for the year on your P&L won't actually be equal to the difference between the retained profit figures on your opening and closing balance sheets?

True, unfortunately.

Putting it another way, some of the profit you have made on the building does show up in the P&L and some doesn't, depending on what value you put on it when revaluing it? If you had never revalued it, all the profit would show up in the P&L?

Absolutely right. I don't think it makes it easy for people, to be honest, but those are the rules.

Intangible fixed assets

Intangible fixed assets are, as the name implies again, assets which you can't touch. In other words, they are things like patents, copyrights, brand names, trademarks, etc.

There are two big differences between tangible and intangible fixed assets.

- If you buy a fixed asset, you know what you paid for it, whether it is tangible or intangible. If you build a tangible asset yourself, you can still calculate the cost fairly accurately. It is very difficult, however, to calculate the cost of many intangible assets like brand names and patents, which are developed internally, sometimes over a long period of time.

- While it is not always easy to assess the useful life of a tangible asset, it is certainly a lot easier in most cases than for intangible assets like brand names.

We account for intangible assets as follows:

- If the intangible asset was bought, then it should be treated as a fixed asset and it should be amortised like goodwill over its economic life. If that life is considered by the company to be greater than 20 years, annual impairment reviews are required.

- If an intangible asset is generated by company internally, then it should be treated as a fixed asset and amortised as such *only if* it has a readily ascertainable market value. Otherwise, the costs of generating the asset should be treated as normal operating costs.

Leases

A lease is a contract between the owner of an asset (such as a building, a car, a photocopier) and someone who wants the use of that asset for

a period of time. The owner of the asset is known as the **lessor**; the user of the asset is the **lessee**.

For accounting purposes, leases are divided into two sorts: **operating leases** and **finance leases**.

Operating leases

An operating lease is one where the lessee pays the lessor a rental for using the asset for a period of time that is normally substantially less than the useful life of the asset. The lessor retains most of the risks and rewards of owning the asset. A typical example would be renting a telephone system for six months.

Accounting for an operating lease is easy. You simply recognise the rental payments as they fall due. Thus you would reduce retained profit and reduce cash for each rental payment. Typically the notes to the accounts would show how long operating leases have to run and what the total of the next twelve months' payments is.

Finance leases

A finance lease is one where the lessee uses the asset for the vast majority of the asset's useful life. In such circumstances the lessee has most of the risks and rewards of ownership. A typical example would be a car lease. We account for finance leases in a different way from operating leases.

Let's assume you need a car that would cost £10,000 to buy outright. Instead of leasing it, you could obtain a loan from your bank and buy the car. If you did this, your balance sheet would show a fixed asset of £10,000 and a liability to the bank of £10,000. You would then treat the fixed asset and the loan exactly as you would any other fixed asset and loan. You would depreciate the asset at an appropriate rate, and you would pay interest on the loan. At some point you would repay the loan.

Acquiring the car this way recognises both the asset and the liability to the bank on your balance sheet. On the other hand, if you lease the car and treat it as an operating lease, neither the asset nor the liability would show up on the balance sheet. You would merely recognise each lease payment by reducing cash and reducing retained profit, as and when the payments were made.

Having such a lease and treating it like an operating lease is what is known as **off-balance sheet finance**, because you are effectively getting a loan to buy an asset without showing either on your balance sheet. As a result, companies can build up substantial liabilities without them appearing on their balance sheets. When we account for finance leases, we therefore make them look like a loan and an asset purchase in two separate transactions.

I understand the principle, but I don't see how the accounting works. Can you explain it in a bit more detail?

The best thing to do is to look at an example. Let's assume that you agree to pay the lessor £300 per month for 48 months to lease a £10,000 car. You would be agreeing to pay a total of £14,400 to the lessor during the life of the lease. Effectively, the lessor has lent you £10,000 (the price of the car), which you have to repay in instalments with interest of £4,400 over 48 months.

You therefore put the asset on the balance sheet at £10,000 and recognise a liability to the lessor of £10,000. The asset you depreciate just as you would any other asset. The lease payments are treated as two separate items. Some of each £300 payment is treated as repayment of the £10,000 'loan' and therefore reduces the liability; the rest of each payment is treated as interest on the loan and reduces retained profit. At the end of 48 months, you have paid the £14,400.

How do you know how much of each payment is repayment of the loan and how much is interest?

This is where it can get a touch complicated. You work it out so that the effective interest rate on what you have left to repay of the loan is always the same. You only really need to understand how to do this if you are actually going to produce your own accounts and you have some finance leases.

What *you* need to understand is what it means when you see:

- 'Lease liability' on the balance sheet. This is the amount of the £10,000 'loan' left to pay.

- 'Interest element of finance leases' in the P&L and cash flow statement. This is the part of the year's lease payments that relate to interest on the £10,000 'loan'.

- 'Capital element of finance leases' in the cash flow statement. This is the part of the year's lease payments that relate to repayment of the principal of the £10,000 'loan'.

Corporation tax

There is one aspect of corporation tax that you will regularly encounter in company accounts, but which did not appear in Wingate's accounts.

Deferred tax

As I said when we talked about tax in the last session, taxable income is usually different from profit before tax. Frequently, this is because the Inland Revenue make adjustments which, while they reduce the taxable income in the current year, will increase it in future years. In other words, the amount of tax to pay does not change but the timing of the payment does.

In such cases, companies allow for the fact that they may have to pay this extra tax some time (which can be several years) in the future, by recognising a liability to the taxman called **deferred tax**. You will see this on balance sheets under long-term liabilities. It is really no different from corporation tax, otherwise. Sometimes it works the other way around and companies pay more tax now than you might expect from their profits and less in future. In this case, the company would have a deferred tax asset.

Exchange gains and losses

Many major companies have dealings abroad which involve them in foreign currencies. There are two principal ways in which a company can be affected by foreign currencies:

- The company trades with third parties, making transactions which are denominated in foreign currencies.

- The company owns all or part of a business which is based abroad and which keeps its accounts in a foreign currency.

Let's have a brief look at each in turn.

Trading in foreign currencies

Suppose you sold some products to a customer in the USA for $7,000 to be paid ninety days after the date of the transaction. You would translate the $7,000 into pounds sterling at the exchange rate prevailing on the day of the transaction and enter the transaction in your accounts. Assume the exchange rate was $1.75 to the pound; this would make the $7,000 worth £4,000.

When the American customer pays (ninety days later), the exchange rate is likely to be different. Assume it is $1.60 per £; this would mean that the customer is effectively paying you £4,375, when your accounts say you should be getting £4,000. By waiting ninety days to be paid, you have made a profit of £375.

This profit is known as an exchange gain. Naturally, if the exchange rate had gone the other way, you would have made an exchange loss. If these exchange gains or losses are material, they will be disclosed in the accounts of the company.

Presumably, if a large proportion of your sales are overseas, your profits could be substantially affected by exchange gains or losses?

Yes, it's a major issue for some companies. Such companies employ people in their finance departments to **hedge** the exposure. This means creating an exposure to the foreign currency in a way that is equal and opposite to the exposure you have from the original transaction. Then, whatever happens to the exchange rate, you should end up with the same amount of money in your own currency.

You would be surprised, however, how many companies choose not to hedge their exposure, in the hope of making an exchange gain. Effectively they are speculating on the currency markets. This is what banks have whole departments doing twenty-four hours a day! Ordinary companies really should not be trying to beat the banks at their own game – they won't be able to in the long run and are virtually certain to end up making more losses than gains.

Owning foreign businesses

If you have a subsidiary in a foreign country then, when you consolidate its accounts with yours, you have to translate the figures from the foreign currency into your own. This translation is usually made at the rate of exchange on the date of the balance sheet.

Since the exchange rate is likely to move during the year, then, even if the foreign subsidiary's balance sheet didn't change during the year, the figures you include in your consolidated accounts for the subsidiary will be different from those at the start of the year. This, too, is known as an exchange gain or loss. This exchange gain or loss does not show up on the P&L, however, since it would distort the actual trading performance of the company. Instead, the exchange gain or loss is shown as a separate adjustment in shareholders' equity. The notes to the accounts will identify the size of the adjustments made.

Fully diluted earnings per share

When we were looking at Wingate, we saw that earnings per share was simply the profit for the year divided by the weighted average number of shares in issue during the year.

On some companies' accounts, you will see an additional line on the P&L called **fully diluted earnings per share**.

This calculation arises when a company has given someone the right to have shares issued to them. We have looked at three examples in this session:

- Convertible bonds
- Convertible preference shares
- Options

If the company has issued any of these instruments, then it might find it suddenly has to issue some new shares; the current shareholders would then own a smaller percentage of the share capital than they did before. Fully diluted earnings per share are calculated by assuming that all the people who hold rights to have shares issued to them had exercised those rights at the *beginning* of the year.

It is not as simple, however, as just adding the extra shares to the number of shares currently in issue and dividing that into the earnings, because the act of converting into shares changes the earnings. For example, if the convertible bond holders had converted at the beginning of the year, the company would not have had to pay them interest for the year.

Can you show us an example?

Assume a company has issued £1.5m worth of convertible bonds with a coupon of 10 per cent. Every £3 of the bonds can be converted into one ordinary share. The company made an operating profit of £400k and pays tax at a rate of 30 per cent of profit before tax. Before conversion of the bonds, the company has one million shares.

The earnings per share calculations are shown in Table 7.1. As you can see, the earnings per share actually rise on conversion of the bonds, due to the reduction in the interest being paid. Depending on a company's circumstances, earnings per share can rise or fall when dilution is calculated, although typically they fall.

If you're calculating fully diluted earnings per share for a company which has issued some options, presumably there is no interest saving and thus no adjustment needed to the earnings?

It's true that there is no interest saving, but when an option is exercised, the exercise price has to be paid to the company in return for the new share. If an option had been exercised at the beginning of a particular year, the company would have had some extra cash for the whole year on which it could have earned interest. We could therefore estimate this interest (which we call **notional interest**) and adjust our earnings figure appropriately before calculating dilution. As it happens, this is not the way it is done. The approved method involves calculations relating to the fair value of the shares to which the options relate. This achieves the same thing but is a bit complicated and we don't really have time to go into it now.

£'000	Bond not converted	Bond converted
Amount of bond	1,500	
Coupon	10%	
Conversion rate		£3.00
Operating profit	400	400
Interest on bond	(150)	–
Profit before tax	250	400
Tax at 30%	(75)	(120)
Profit after tax	175	280
Number of shares	1.0m	1.5m
Earnings per share	17.5p	18.7p

Table 7.1 Calculation of earnings per share dilution

We have now done enough accounting. It's time to move on to financial analysis, which is what gives us real insight into a company. Before we do that, though, let me recap on this session.

SUMMARY

- In this session we have seen a number of slightly more sophisticated features of company accounts.

- None of these features, taken alone, is particularly difficult to understand – it is the combination of many such features that make company accounts look complicated.

- The secret, as I have said before, is always to look at the effect of a transaction on the balance sheet, remembering always that there must be at least two entries.

- Then, if the transaction affects retained profit, you know it will affect the P&L. If it affects cash, you know it will affect the cash flow statement.

You can't escape the fact that shareholders have invested money in the hope of a good return, relative to the risk they have taken. This has to be our guiding principle when we analyse a company's performance.

Financial analysis – introduction

- The ultimate goal
- Two components of a company
- The general approach to financial analysis
- Wingate's highlights
- Summary

Up to now, all our sessions have been about accounting. You should now be able to read most companies' annual reports and understand them. This does not mean, though, that the accounts *tell* you anything. That is where financial analysis comes in.

This weekend came about partly because Tom is worried about Wingate's financial position. The managing director would have you believe that things are going pretty well for Wingate – sales, profits and dividends are all rising steadily. However, Tom's perception is that the company is expansion crazy, cutting prices and giving very generous payment terms so as to win new contracts. What's more, the company has been spending a lot of money on new premises, etc.

I have had a look at Wingate in some detail. In fact, I've gone back over the last five years' accounts and discovered one or two interesting things. Before we go into that, though, I want to cover three very important aspects of financial analysis:

- First, I want to make sure we all understand the ultimate financial goal of a company; what is a company trying to achieve?

- Then I want to be sure that you really understand the distinction between the two components of a company – the enterprise and the funding structure.

- Finally, I will outline the general approach we take to financial analysis.

At the end of this session, I'll show you some graphs of Wingate's sales, profits and dividends which, as Tom said, do paint a fairly rosy picture. We'll then take a break and in the next session have a look and see how rosy the picture really is.

The ultimate goal

If I gave you £100 and told you to invest it, you would have a choice of many places to put that £100. For example:

1. You could buy £100 worth of tickets in the lottery.

2. You could put it all on the outsider in the 2.30pm race at Newmarket.

3. You could buy some shares in a new company set up to engage in oil exploration.

4. You could buy shares in one of the top 100 companies in Britain.

5. You could put it in a deposit account at one of the big high street banks.

Two things should strike you as you go down this list:

- First, the choices become less risky. With number 1, you are extremely likely to lose all your money. With number 5 you are almost certain to get all your money back plus some interest.

- Second, the potential return (or profit) on your £100 investment gets lower. If you win the lottery, you will make millions of pounds in a matter of days. If you put the money in the bank you will earn less than £10 interest, even if you leave your £100 there for a year.

The point is that, generally, people will not take risks unless there is some reward (or potential reward) for doing so. The greater the risk, the greater the potential reward people require.

Although we could have a long philosophical debate about the role of companies in society, you can't escape the fact that the shareholders have invested money in the hope of a good return, relative to the risk they have taken. This has to be our guiding principle when we analyse a company's performance.

How high the return should be depends on the risk of the investment. Measuring risk is extremely difficult and well beyond what we can hope to cover today. What we can say, though, is that the return must be higher than we could obtain by putting the same amount of money on deposit in a high street bank, since we could do that with virtually no risk. What we can get on deposit in a bank will depend on the economic circumstances at the time, but I tend to use 5 per cent per annum (before tax) as a simple benchmark.

So the directors of Wingate should be looking simply to maximise the return on the money invested in the business?

In principle, yes, but with two very important qualifications.

The long-term perspective

Some companies could easily increase the return they provide on the money invested in the business. Let's say you run a long-established company which has a dominant market share in its industry. By raising your prices, you are likely, in the short term, to raise your profits and hence the return to shareholders. In the longer term, however, customers will start to buy from your competitors and, sooner or later, you

will have lost so much business that your profits will be lower than they were before you raised your prices.

The point is obvious. Short-term gains can have high long-term costs. Directors have to make that trade-off on behalf of their shareholders.

Liquidity

The second qualification relates to the trade-off between cash flow and profitability, which is something that applies to individuals as well as companies. Assume you have £500 which you want to put on deposit at the bank. You can put it in an ordinary deposit account which pays you interest of, say, 4 per cent per annum. The bank manager, however, suggests that you put the money in a special account which will pay you 6 per cent per annum. The only condition of this special account is that you have to leave your money in the account for the whole year.

Obviously, the special account would provide you with a higher return than the ordinary deposit account. But if you have to pay the final balance on your summer holiday in two months' time and therefore need that £500 then, you would have to opt for the ordinary deposit account and accept a lower return.

Companies have all sorts of opportunities to make similar trade-offs between profit and cash flow. The most obvious relates to the terms on which they buy and sell goods. Many companies offer a discount for rapid payment, others charge a premium for giving extended credit.

Liquidity is the ability to pay your short-term liabilities. You can always get a higher return if you are prepared to reduce your liquidity. If you go too far, however, you will be unable to pay your debts on time and will go bust.

So what you're saying is that the main objective of a company is to maximise the return it provides on the money invested, based on an appropriate trade-off botwoon tho short and long torm porspoctivos, whilo onsuring that tho business remains liquid?

Exactly.

The two components of a company

When I was explaining how we draw up a P&L and cash flow statement in one of our earlier sessions, I made the distinction between the **operations** and the **funding structure** of a company. This distinction is absolutely crucial to meaningful financial analysis and it is essential that you really understand it. Can I work on that assumption?

I think you had better go over it again, Chris.

The simple view of a company

OK. Let's look at what a company does, in the simplest terms:

1. It raises funds from shareholders and by borrowing from banks.

2. It then uses this cash to trade, which involves doing some of the following things:

   - buying (and selling) fixed assets
   - buying raw materials
   - manufacturing products
   - selling products and services
   - paying employees, suppliers
   - collecting cash from customers
   - etc.

3. If trading is successful, then the company makes a pay-out to the people who funded the business. First, the bank has to be paid interest on its loans. Any remaining profit belongs to the shareholders, although the Inland Revenue demands a cut.

This is a pretty simple view of a business, but, in a nutshell, that's what goes on.

The point to notice is that the activities in the middle [see 2 above] are completely unaffected by *how* the funding was split between the different sources. A company needs a certain amount of funding in order to trade but the source of those funds is irrelevant. This bit in the middle, which is the underlying business or operation of the company, we call the **enterprise**.

The source of the funds does affect the share of the profit that goes to the bank rather than the shareholders and the taxman. The more debt (i.e. overdraft, loans, etc.) a company has, the more interest it will have to pay and the less there will be for the taxman and the shareholders. The way in which the funding is made up we call the **funding structure**.

I can see the principle, but I'm not sure how it relates to the financial statements. Presumably it does?

Yes, and it's actually very easy. Let's look at the balance sheet first. If we go back to our model balance sheet [Figure 8.1], we can assign all the items into one of the two categories. I have shaded all those that are part of the funding structure. If you study the chart, you will see that all the unshaded items are unaffected by the funding structure.

You've shaded the cash box, implying that it is part of the funding structure. Surely cash is not affected by the source of the funding?

No, but if you have got cash on your balance sheet, then effectively you've just got less of an overdraft. Hence we 'net the cash off' the overdraft (or bank loans).

Why have you got social security and other taxes included as part of the enterprise? I thought you said that taxes were part of the funding structure.

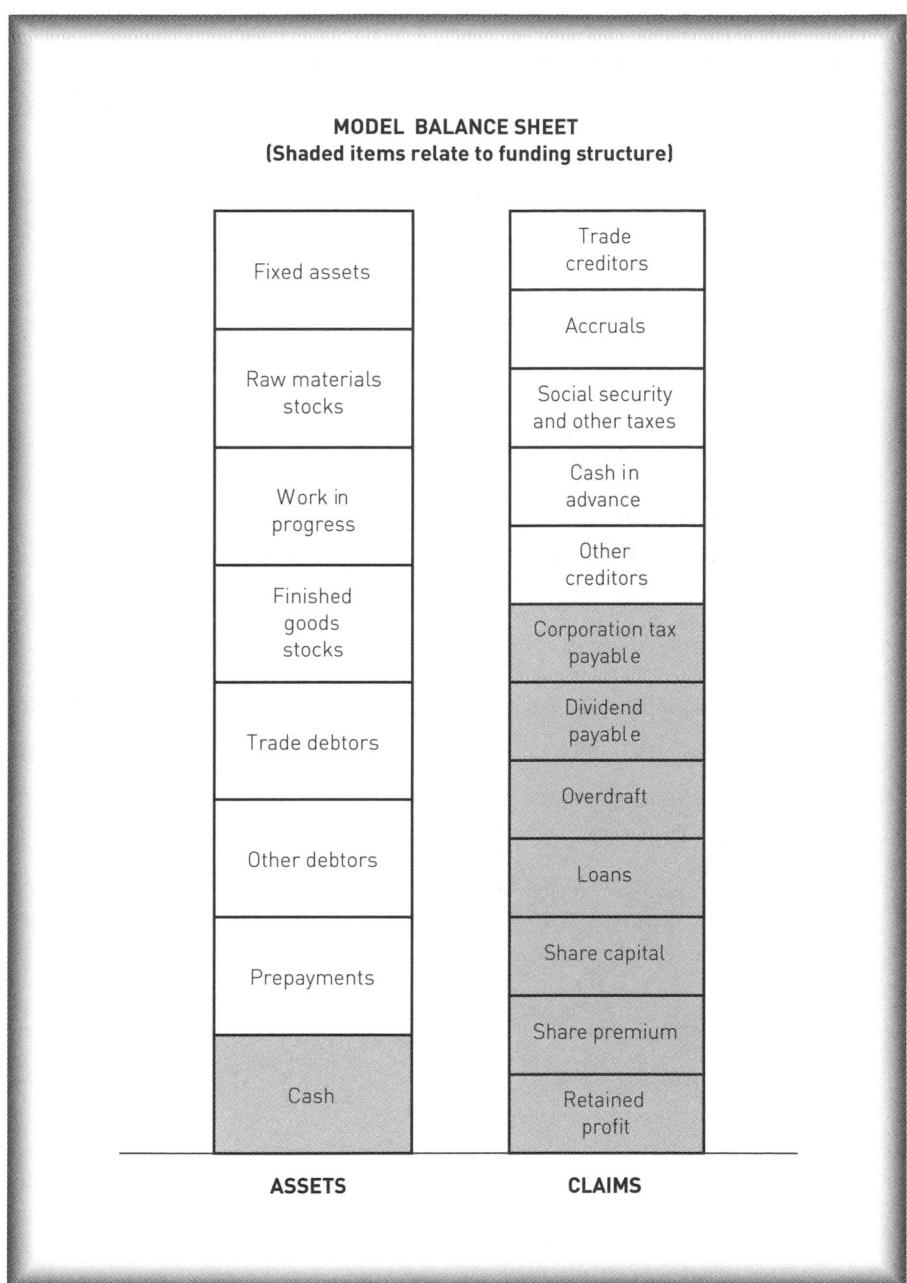

Figure 8.1 Model balance sheet chart distinguishing the funding structure from the enterprise

That question is a perfect example of not applying the principle correctly. Social security, VAT, etc. are taxes that are determined by things to do with the underlying business, like how much you sell, how much you buy, how many employees you have and how much you pay them. These taxes are *not* affected by the source of the funds, so they must be part of the enterprise.

Corporation tax is calculated after paying interest on debt. The more interest paid, the lower the tax to pay. Hence corporation tax is affected by the amount of debt; in other words, it is affected by the source of the funding and is therefore part of the funding structure.

The balance sheet rearranged

We can actually rearrange the balance sheet to make it distinguish the enterprise from the funding structure. It's just a matter of moving certain items from one side of our balance sheet equation to the other.

As an example, look at the trade creditors box at the top of the claims bar on the balance sheet chart. We could remove this box from the claims bar and subtract the same amount from, say, the trade debtors box on the assets bar. We might then change the name of this box to 'Trade debtors minus trade creditors'. Because we have subtracted the trade creditors from both bars of our balance sheet, the balance sheet still balances.

To distinguish between the enterprise and the funding structure, we make the following adjustments to the balance sheet chart and come up with the rearranged version [Figure 8.2].

1. Leave the fixed assets box as it is, but take all the other items relating to the enterprise and combine them into one box which we will call **working capital**. What we get is:

> Working capital = Raw materials stocks
> + Work in progress
> + Finished goods stocks
> + Trade debtors
> + Other debtors
> + Prepayments
> – Trade creditors
> – Accruals
> – Social security and other taxes
> – Cash in advance
> – Other creditors

*What **is** working capital though? You don't go out and buy it the way you do fixed assets, do you?*

Obviously not. Working capital is money you need to operate. Think of it as cash you would have in your bank account if you did not have to hold stocks, give credit to customers, make prepayments, etc. The fact that you do have to do these things means that you need to 'invest' cash in working capital.

2. The next thing we need to sort out is the cash at the bottom of the assets bar.

   As we have discussed, having cash really just means you have got less of an overdraft or bank loan, since you could just pay either of them off with the spare cash. In rearranging our balance sheet, therefore, all we do is create a new box called **net debt**. This is the sum of all the debt of the company after subtracting any cash.

3. When we were looking at Wingate, we saw that shareholders' equity, which is the share of the company's assets 'due' to the shareholders, was made up of share capital, share premium and retained profit. If

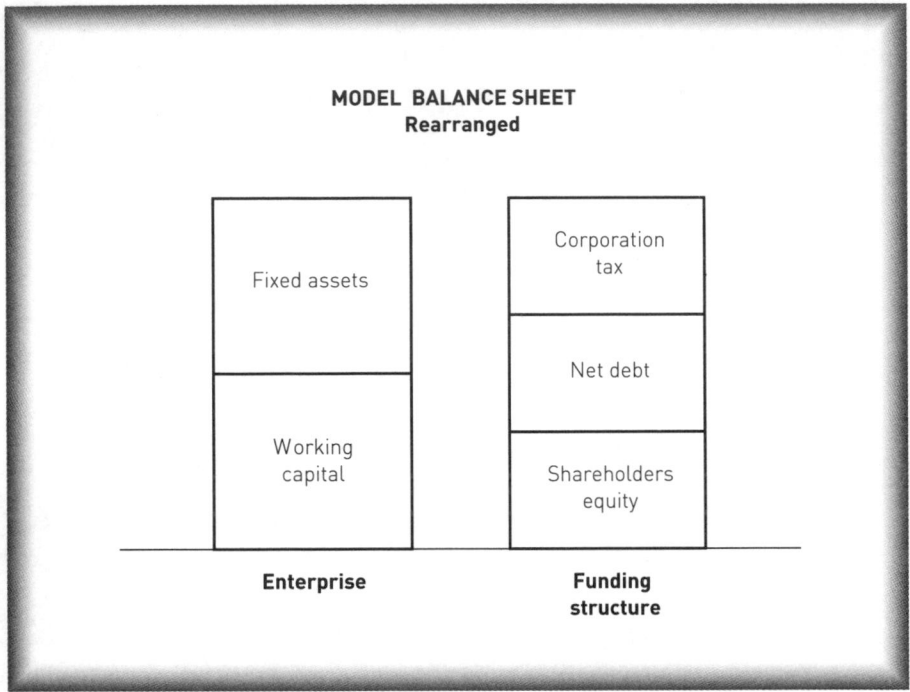

Figure 8.2 Model balance sheet chart rearranged

you think about it, dividends payable should also be included under shareholders' equity as they represent money due to the shareholders' which is actually going to be paid in the near future.

*So why **aren't** dividends payable included under shareholders' equity?*

Because, once a dividend has been declared by the directors of a company, it becomes a current liability like any other current liability and has to be shown as such.

For the purposes of financial analysis, we do include dividends payable in shareholders' equity, which therefore represents the total funding for the company provided by the shareholders. **Shareholders' equity** thus becomes a separate box on our rearranged balance sheet.

Why are dividends payable and retained profit part of the funding provided by the shareholders? Surely the only actual money they have provided is the share capital plus the share premium.

That's true, but being owed money by a company is the same as having put that money into the company. Dividends payable and retained profit both represent money that is 'due' to the shareholders. If you like, think of the company paying out to the shareholders everything they are due and the shareholders immediately putting the money back into the company.

4. The only other thing we haven't dealt with is corporation tax. This is the same as the dividends and retained profit, in a sense. The Inland Revenue have not actually put money into the company, but by not taking what they are owed immediately, they are effectively funding the company.

   We therefore leave the corporation tax in a box of its own as part of the funding structure.

If you now look at the rearranged balance sheet, you will see that it shows clearly:

- The sources of the funding for the business
- The uses of that funding.

Wingate's rearranged balance sheet

We can rearrange Wingate's balance sheet at the end of year five to look like this. It will make our analysis much quicker and easier if we actually write it out now [Table 8.1]. As you can see, it has all the same numbers in it as before and it still balances.

WINGATE FOODS PLC

Rearranged balance sheet at end of year five

		£'000
Enterprise		
Fixed assets		5,326
Working capital		
Stocks		
Raw materials	362	
Work in progress	17	
Finished goods	862	
Total stocks		1,241
Debtors		
Trade debtors	1,437	
Prepayments	88	
Other debtors	36	
Total debtors		1,561
Creditors		
Trade creditors	(850)	
Soc sec/other taxes	(140)	
Accruals	(113)	
Cash in advance	(20)	
Total creditors	(1,123)	
Net working capital		1,679
Net operating assets		7,005
Funding structure		
Taxation		202
Net debt		
Cash	(15)	
Overdraft	893	
Loans	3,000	
Net debt		3,878
Shareholders' equity		
Dividends payable	154	
Share capital	50	
Share premium	275	
Retained profit	2,446	
Total shareholders' equity		2,925
Net funding		7,005

Table 8.1 Wingate's rearranged balance sheet at end of year five

Wingate's P&L

Distinguishing between the enterprise and the funding structure on the P&L is extremely simple. All the items down to operating profit are part of the enterprise. None of them would be affected by a change in the funding structure. Operating profit is the profit made from operating the assets, as you would expect.

All the items after operating profit such as interest, tax, dividends are all related to the funding structure.

Wingate's cash flow statement

Similarly, if you look at the cash flow statement on pages 280–281, you will see that the six different headings fall into one or other of our two categories: 'Operating activities' and 'Capital expenditure' relate to the enterprise; 'Returns on investments and servicing of finance', 'Taxation', 'Equity dividends paid' and 'Financing' relate to the funding structure.

I think I'm getting the idea, but what's the point of this distinction?

The point is simple but important. The enterprise represents the actual *business* of the company. The funding structure represents the way the directors have chosen to raise the necessary funds. By making this distinction we can:

- Assess the performance of the business without the sources of the funding confusing the picture.

- Analyse the implications for both shareholders and lenders of the way the company has been funded.

The general approach to financial analysis

Even when you understand how a company's accounts are put together, there is still an alarming profusion of numbers. You can't just sit down and read company accounts as you would a novel. You have to use them like a dictionary – look up the things you are interested in.

There are three basic steps in any financial analysis:

- Choose the parameter that interests you.
- Look it up (and calculate it if necessary).
- Interpret it and, hopefully, gain some insight into the company.

By parameter I mean any measure that tells you something about a company's performance. There are certain useful parameters that you can read straight from the accounts, the most obvious example being sales. In general, however, the most useful parameters are ratios of one item in the accounts to another.

Interpretation of parameters

There are two ways to go about interpreting parameters:

- Trend analysis
- Benchmarking

Trend analysis is looking at how a given parameter has changed over a period of time. Trends can tell you a lot about the way a company is being managed and can help you to anticipate future performance. Usually, we look at such trends over a five-year timeframe.

Benchmarking means comparing a parameter at a point in time with the same parameters of competitors or against universal standards (such as the interest rate on deposit accounts).

Benchmarking against competitors is particularly useful for assessing the relative strength of companies in the same industry.

This is another reason we distinguish between the enterprise and the funding structure. Companies in the same industry might have very different funding structures. Some might have no debt at all, others may have a lot. If you are interested in comparing the way they run their underlying business, the funding structure is irrelevant.

Even when benchmarking against competitors, the best approach is to look at trends in parameters rather than a point in time. It is substantially more work, but will give a more reliable picture of how the companies are performing relative to one another.

Wingate's highlights

We are now more or less ready to start our analysis of Wingate's accounts. Before we do, let's look at the parameters that the management seem to be focusing on. These are sales, operating profit, profit before tax and dividends. I have drawn graphs of each of these parameters over the last five years [Figures 8.3 to 8.6].

Based on these parameters, you can see why the management can claim to be doing a reasonable job. All four parameters are rising steadily. The question, of course, is whether these are the right parameters to be looking at.

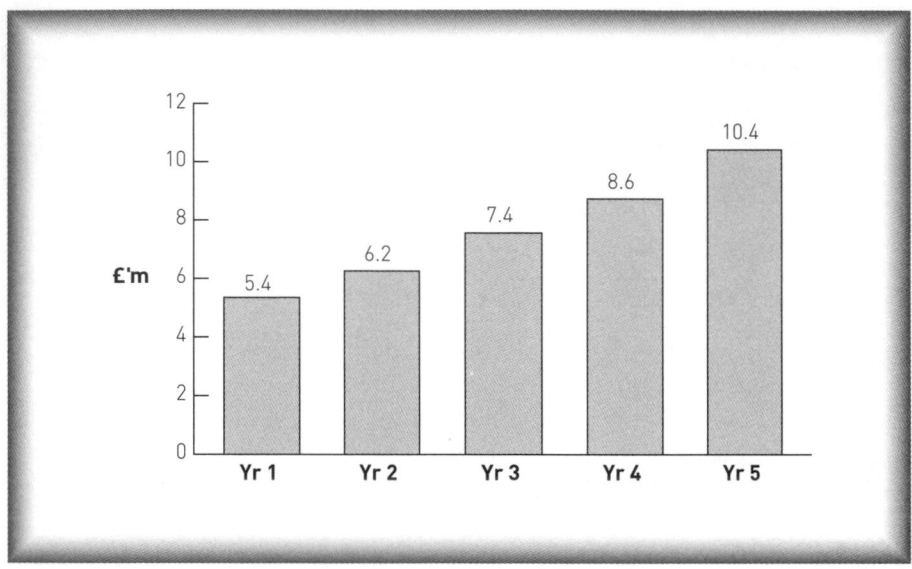

Figure 8.3 Wingate's sales (years 1–5)

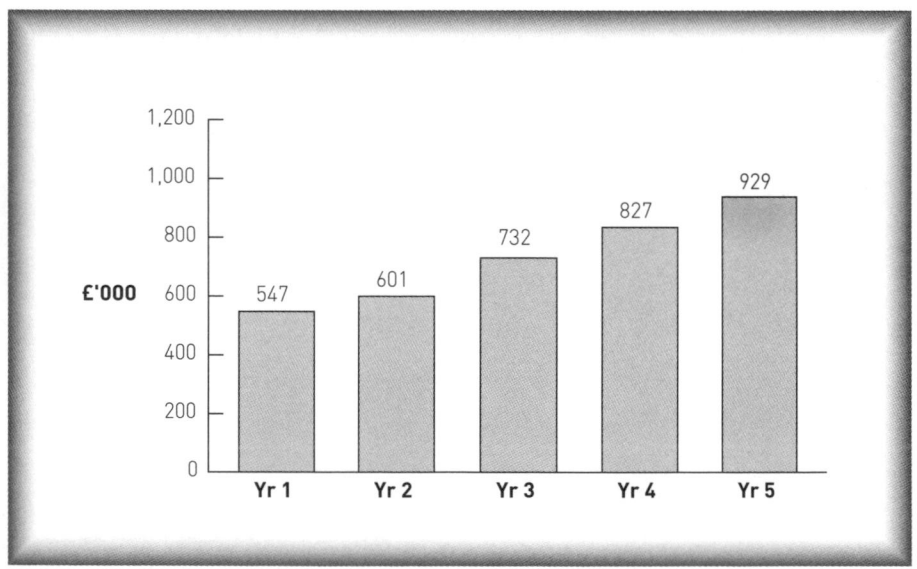

Figure 8.4 Wingate's operating profit (years 1–5)

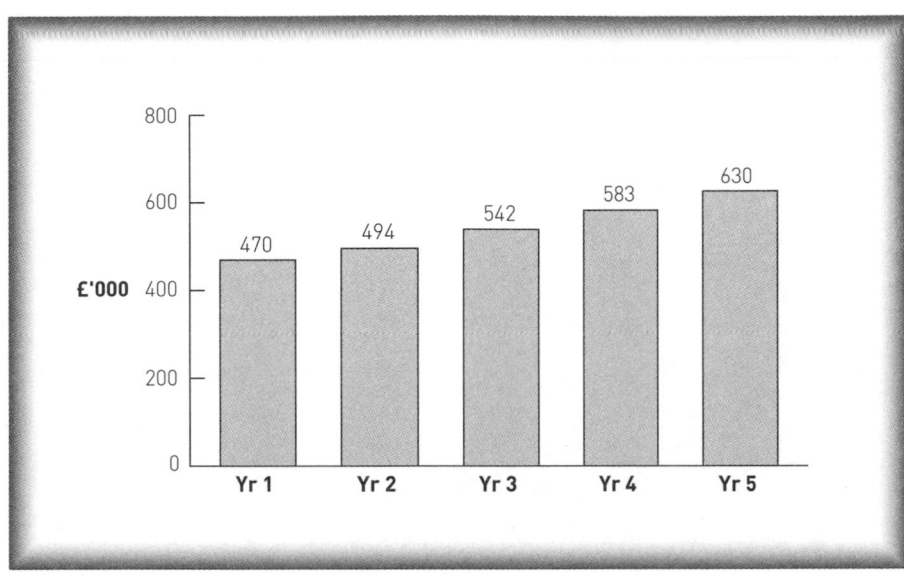

Figure 8.5 Wingate's profit before tax (years 1–5)

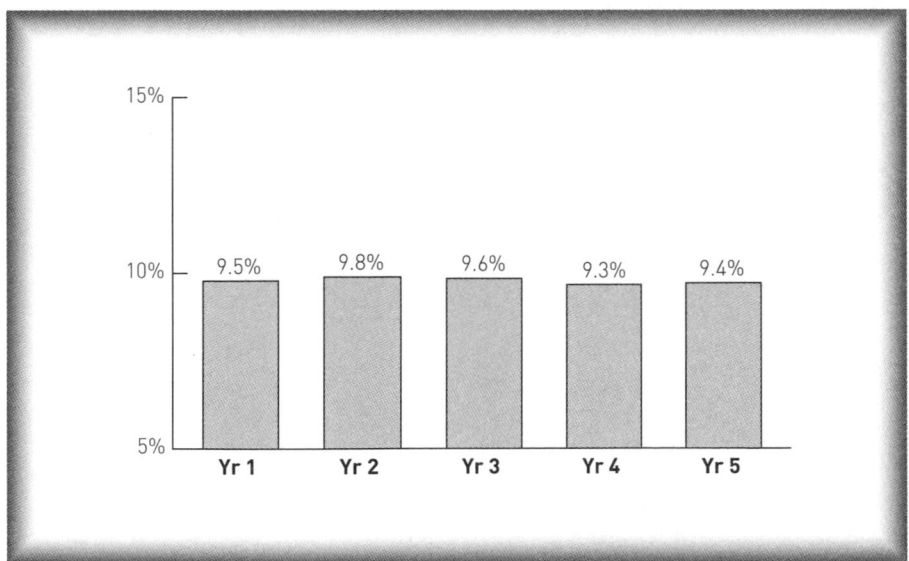

Figure 8.6 Wingate's dividends (years 1–5)

SUMMARY

- In general, the greater the risk of an investment, the greater must be the potential reward. Otherwise, people will simply not take the risk.

- Companies must therefore offer a reward (or 'return') which is commensurate with the risk to the investor.

- The financial objective of a company is to maximise the return on the money invested in it, while making appropriate trade-offs between:
  - the short- and long-term perspectives
  - profitability and liquidity

- From a financial viewpoint, we can distinguish between the enterprise and the funding structure of a company. This distinction enables us to do three things:
  - to assess how the actual business of a company is performing without the sources of the funding confusing the picture
  - to make more meaningful comparisons of a business with competitors
  - to analyse the implications for both shareholders and lenders of the way the company has been funded

- Financial analysis requires the selection and calculation of a number of relevant parameters. These parameters can then be interpreted by observing trends over a period of time or by benchmarking.

What I'm going to do first is show you how we
calculate the return that the enterprise is providing
and see how it has changed over the last five years.
We will then ask ourselves why this has happened.
This will lead on to a variety of other analyses.

Analysis of the enterprise

- Return on capital employed (ROCE)
- The components of ROCE
- Where do we go from here?
- Expense ratios
- Capital ratios
- Summary

We are now ready to start looking in depth at Wingate's financial performance, starting with the enterprise.

What I'm going to do first is show you how we calculate the return that the enterprise is providing and see how it has changed over the last five years. We will then ask ourselves why this has happened. This will lead us on to a variety of other analyses, which will provide greater insight into Wingate's true financial performance.

Return on capital employed

When we rearranged our balance sheet to distinguish between the enterprise and the funding structure, we ended up with one side of our balance sheet showing the **net operating assets** of the business. This is the amount of money that is invested in the operation. The managers of the business are trying to make as high a return on this money as possible (or at least they should be). Net operating assets are also known as **capital employed** – the amount of capital that is employed in the operation. The measure of performance is thus usually known as **return on capital employed** ('**ROCE**' for short).

Calculating ROCE

Since we have already rearranged Wingate's balance sheet for the end of year five (see page 160), we know the capital employed is just the net operating assets as shown in the balance sheet, i.e. £7,005k.

We also know that the return is the profit made by operating those assets. This is the operating profit, which we can read directly off the P&L as being £929k in year five.

Thus the return on capital employed is as follows:

$$929 / 7,005 = 13.3\%$$

What I want you to do now is to work out the ROCE for the previous year. The figures are all there, alongside the figures I used to do year five. I suggest that you actually rearrange the balance sheet at the end of year four, as I did for year five. When you become more practised at doing these types of analyses, you will just read the appropriate figures from the balance sheet and the notes, but it is easy to miss something if you are not careful.

What you should have got is as follows:

Operating profit = £827k
Capital employed = £5,670k
Return on capital employed = 14.6%

Surprisingly, we got that. I do have a question, though. Why are you using the capital employed at the end of the year? If I put £1,000 in a bank deposit account for a year and earn £40 interest, I would calculate my return based on the £1,000 at the start of the year not the £1,040 I have at the end (i.e. I would say I got a return of 4 per cent, not 3.8 per cent).

Technically, you're right, Sarah. People tend to use the year end figure, though. They do this because capital employed at the end of the year is usually larger than at the start of the year. This means that they get a lower ROCE, which therefore presents a more conservative view of the company.

You can use the capital employed at the start of the year, if you want. You will get slightly different answers, but they are unlikely to change any decisions you will make as a result. Some people use the average of the starting and ending capital employed, on the grounds that the capital employed has been constantly changing throughout the year and the average is therefore a better measure. Whichever approach you take, the most important thing is to be *consistent*. Let's now look at what ROCE tells us.

ROCE vs a benchmark

As we've said before, the whole point of investing in businesses is to make a higher return than we could from putting our cash in a deposit account. Thus the first thing we can do is to compare the ROCE with the interest rate we could get at the bank. If you remember, I suggested using 5 per cent as a crude benchmark.

At 13.3 per cent in year five and 14.6 per cent in year four, the business is certainly outperforming a bank deposit, though not by that much given the relative risks of a bank deposit and a small company's shares. If we had the accounts of some competitors we could compare their ROCE's with Wingate's, which would tell us how they are performing relative to each other.

Trend analysis of ROCE

As we have just seen, ROCE has declined by 1.3 per cent from 14.6 per cent to 13.3 per cent. This difference is not sufficient to enable us to draw any real conclusions. You might well find that a company with two such ROCE figures would achieve, say, 16 per cent next year.

What we do, therefore, is to get old copies of the annual report and look at what has happened over the last few years to see if there is an identifiable trend. I've plotted a graph for you of Wingate's ROCE over the last five years [Figure 9.1].

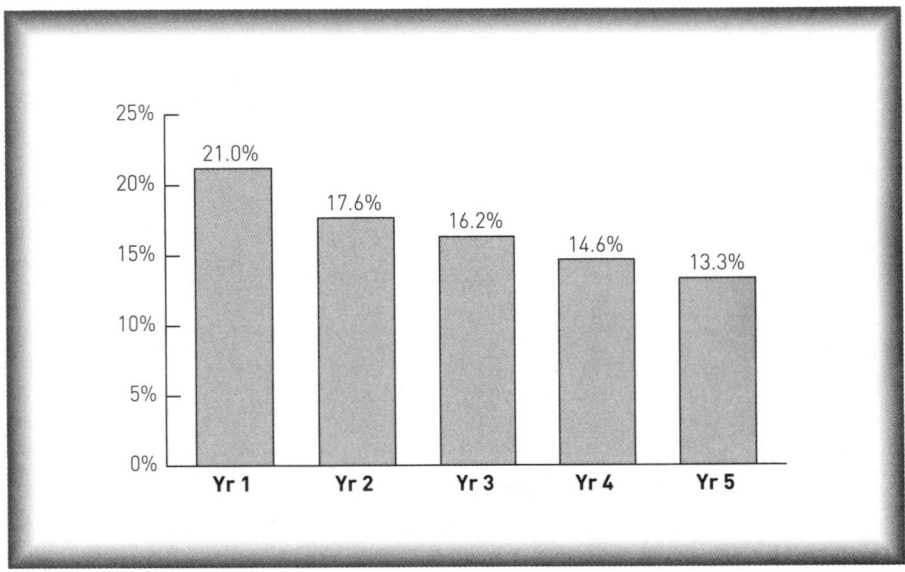

Figure 9.1 Wingate's return on capital employed (years 1–5)

This suggests that the ROCE has gone down drastically, Chris! Are you sure it's right?

It is right and it's pretty worrying. There is a very clear, steep downward trend here. If that keeps going, you are going to end up with a business which is not even giving as high a return as you could get by putting the money in the bank.

But if Wingate's profits grew every year for the last five years, how can ROCE possibly be falling so fast?

This is the whole point of being concerned with profitability rather than profit. Remember that ROCE is profit divided by capital employed.

Although your profit has been growing, the capital employed must have been growing faster. The result is a decline in ROCE.

The components of ROCE

We have discovered that ROCE is declining alarmingly. We now ask ourselves why.

We look at ROCE because we are interested in what profits can be generated from a certain amount of capital employed. What actually happens in a business is that we have a certain amount of capital employed in the operation. Using this capital, we generate sales to customers. These sales in turn lead to profits.

Capital → Sales → Profits

Two pretty obvious questions come out of this:

- How many sales am I getting for every pound of capital employed?
- How much profit am I getting for every pound of sales?

These questions can be answered with two simple ratios.

Capital productivity

The first of these ratios, which tells us how many sales we get from each pound of capital, is called **capital productivity**. To calculate it, we simply take the sales for the year and divide them by the capital employed. Sales for year five were £10,437k and capital employed was £7,005k. Thus we get:

> **Capital productivity** = **Sales / Capital employed**
> = 10,437 / 7,005
> = 1.5

And what exactly is that supposed to tell us, Chris?

Well, not very much, as it stands. We can't really measure it against any universal benchmark, as all industries will be different. We could (and should) compare it with other companies in the industry. What we are trying to understand, though, is why ROCE is falling. Obviously, we should look at capital productivity over the last five years which, you will be glad to know, I have done for you [Figure 9.2].

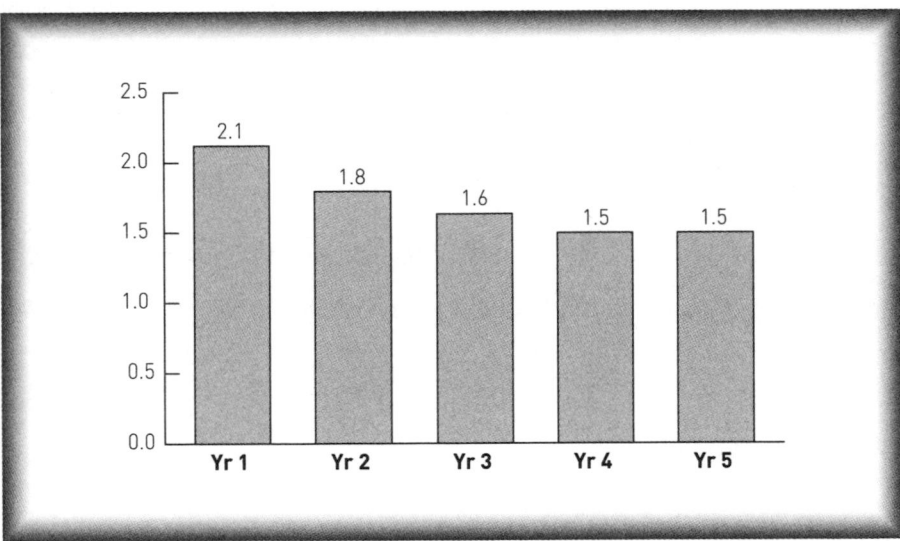

Figure 9.2 Wingate's capital productivity (years 1–5)

As you can see, capital productivity has fallen substantially, although it appears to be levelling off now.

Presumably, we want capital productivity to be as high as possible?

Yes, in principle. The more sales we can get from a given amount of capital the better, but we have to be careful. We are only interested in profitable sales. It's nearly always possible to get more sales out of a given amount of capital just by selling goods very cheaply. The problem with that is that your profit will go down, which is likely to result in your ROCE going down rather than up.

What we should say, therefore, is that, all other things being equal, we want capital productivity to be as high as possible.

Return on sales ('ROS' for short)

We have just seen how we assess the amount of sales we get from a certain amount of capital. The next thing we need to know is how much profit we get from those sales. We calculate this by dividing operating profit by sales. This gives us the following:

> **Return on sales = Operating profit / Sales**
> = 929 / 10,437
> = 8.9%

Wingate's return on sales over five years looks like this [Figure 9.3].

This chart shows some evidence of a downward trend, although not as marked as that of capital productivity. Naturally, with all other things being the same, we want to make as much profit out of each pound of sales as we can, so we want return on sales to be high.

I've absolutely no idea if 9–10 per cent is an acceptable return on sales or not. Are there any universal benchmarks I can use?

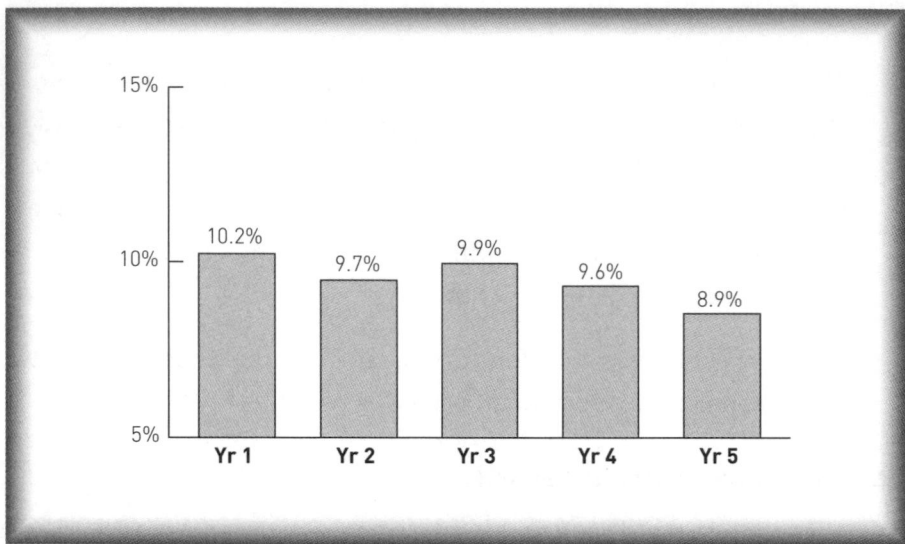

Figure 9.3 Wingate's return on sales (years 1–5)

The answer is no and anyway it's irrelevant. ROCE is the true measure of a company's financial performance. Some of the best retailers have relatively low returns on sales but, because they have high capital productivity, their ROCE is high. You would be much better off owning a company like that than one that had high ROS but low ROCE.

The arithmetic relationship

Hopefully, the logic of going from ROCE to looking at capital productivity and ROS is clear. The relationship between these three ratios can be expressed arithmetically as well:

Profit/CE = Profit/Sales $\times$ Sales/CE

ROCE = ROS x Capital productivity

13.3% = 8.9% x 1.5

Where do we go from here?

So far we have discovered that Wingate's ROCE has fallen substantially. We have also established that this is the result of getting fewer sales for every pound of capital employed and less profit for every pound of sales. Of the two causes, the fall in capital productivity is the more significant.

Naturally, we now ask ourselves why these ratios have declined as they have. We will therefore look at each of the ratios in turn and see what we can find out:

- Since operating profit is what we have left after paying the operating expenses, it obviously makes sense to analyse the operating expenses and see if there is anything we can learn.
- The capital employed in a business is made up of both fixed assets and working capital. Working capital is, in turn, made up of various different elements. We can therefore analyse each of these different elements.

In the same way that we looked at how many sales we got for each pound of assets and how much profit we got for each pound of sales, we will analyse all the expenses and the constituents of capital employed in relation to sales.

Expense ratios

The P&L lists three types of expense: cost of goods sold, distribution and administration. Let's look at these three first.

Cost of goods sold, gross margin

As you will remember, the cost of goods sold ('COGS') is exactly what it says – the cost of buying and/or making the goods to be sold. From the P&L, we know that Wingate's cost of goods sold in year five was

£8,078k. We can therefore divide this by the sales of £10,437k to give us cost of goods sold as a percentage of sales ('COGS%').

$$\begin{aligned} \textbf{COGS \%} \ &\textbf{=} \ \textbf{COGS / Sales} \\ &= \ 8{,}078 \ / \ 10{,}437 \\ &= \ 77.4\% \end{aligned}$$

We also saw earlier that the profit left after subtracting cost of goods sold from sales is known as gross profit. Gross profit as a percentage of sales is known as gross margin.

$$\begin{aligned} \textbf{Gross margin} \ &\textbf{=} \ \textbf{Gross profit / Sales} \\ &= \ 2{,}359 \ / \ 10{,}437 \\ &= \ 22.6\% \end{aligned}$$

Gross margin and the cost of goods sold percentage effectively tell you the same thing. You will find that most people talk about gross margin.

How does this relate to 'mark-up' then, Chris?

If you have something that cost you 77.4 pence and you sell it for £1, your cost of goods is 77.4 per cent and your gross margin is 22.6 per cent, just as we have seen for Wingate. **Mark-up** is the percentage that you add on to your cost to get your selling price, which we calculate by dividing your gross profit by your cost:

Mark-up = Gross profit / Cost
      = 22.6 / 77.4
      = 29.2%

Let's now look at how Wingate's gross margin has changed over the last five years [Figure 9.4].

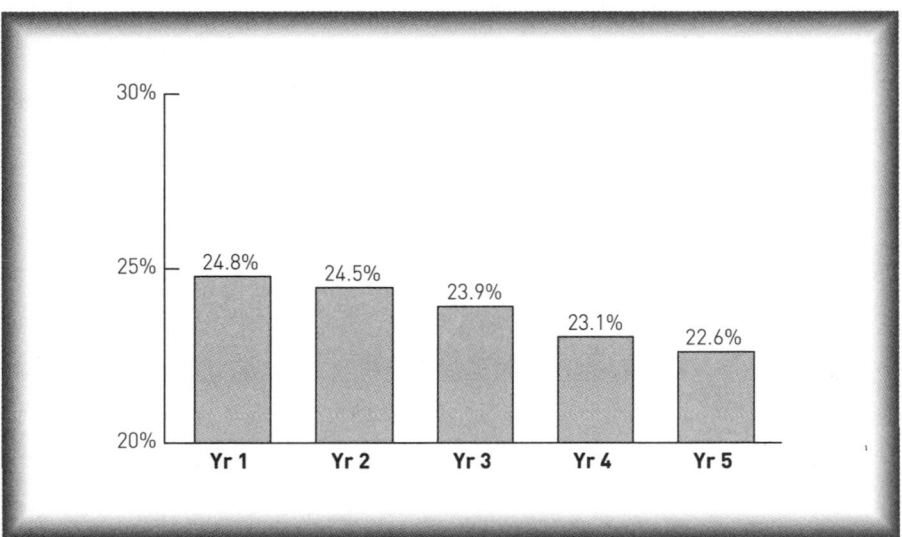

Figure 9.4 Wingate's gross margin (years 1–5)

As you can see, there has been a steady decline in gross margin.

So what this says is that every year a pound's worth of sales is costing us more to produce than the previous year?

Yes, but the way you phrase it makes it sound as if the fault must lie with the director in charge of manufacturing. If the factory is badly run, then you may well be right, but there is an alternative explanation.

What you have to remember with all these analyses is that **sales value** (i.e. the figure for sales in the accounts) is made up of **sales volume** (i.e. the number of packets of biscuits or whatever that you sell) and price (the **price** of each packet of biscuits).

> **Sales value = Sales volume x Price**

Obviously, your cost of manufacturing is not affected by the price you charge your customers, but it is affected by the volume you sell. Take a very simple situation. Assume you sold one million packets of biscuits last year at a price of £1 per packet. These biscuits cost you 70p per packet to produce. What we see is:

Sales	£1m
COGS	£700k
Gross profit	£300k
Gross margin	30%

If, this year, the production director gets the cost of manufacturing down to 65p per packet, but the sales director only manages to sell the same volume of biscuits, despite a lower price of 90p per packet, then we would see:

Sales	£0.9m
COGS	£650k
Gross profit	£250k
Gross margin	28%

So, despite the production director having done a great job, the gross margin has fallen!

The decline in Wingate's gross margin coincides with Tom's tales of the price cuts that the sales department have been making to achieve the growth in sales. Clearly this is more than offsetting any gains they may have made in manufacturing costs. If Wingate is expecting to be able to raise prices once it has won these contracts and built some customer loyalty, then this trend should be reversible. If not, then Wingate had better start manufacturing even more efficiently in the very near future.

Overheads

The other two expenses itemised on Wingate's P&L are distribution and administration. We can calculate these as a percentage of sales, just as we did for cost of goods sold.

Let's look first at distribution. This will include the cost of the sales team as well as the cost of physically transporting the goods to customers. The picture over the five years looks like this [Figure 9.5].

What is interesting about this graph is that it is almost 'flat'. Given the price cutting, this suggests that distribution has become more efficient, which is good.

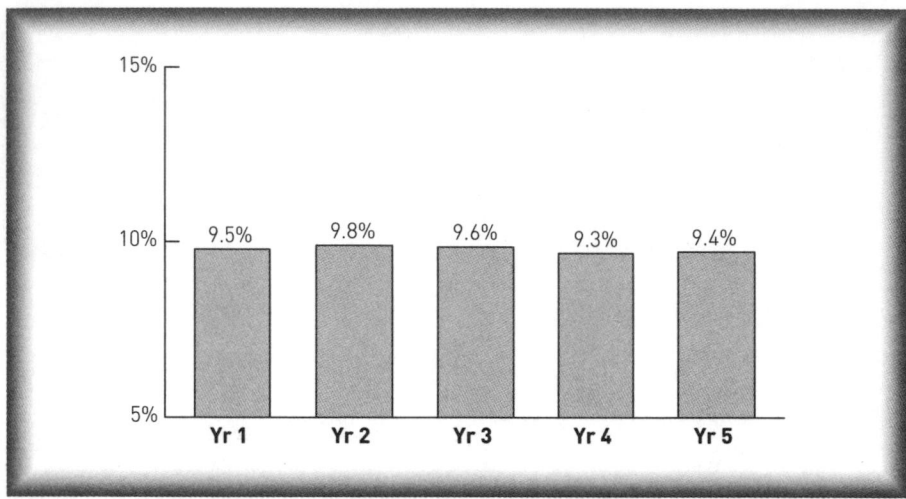

Figure 9.5 Wingate's distribution costs as a percentage of sales (years 1–5)

Administration costs are actually showing a decline relative to sales:

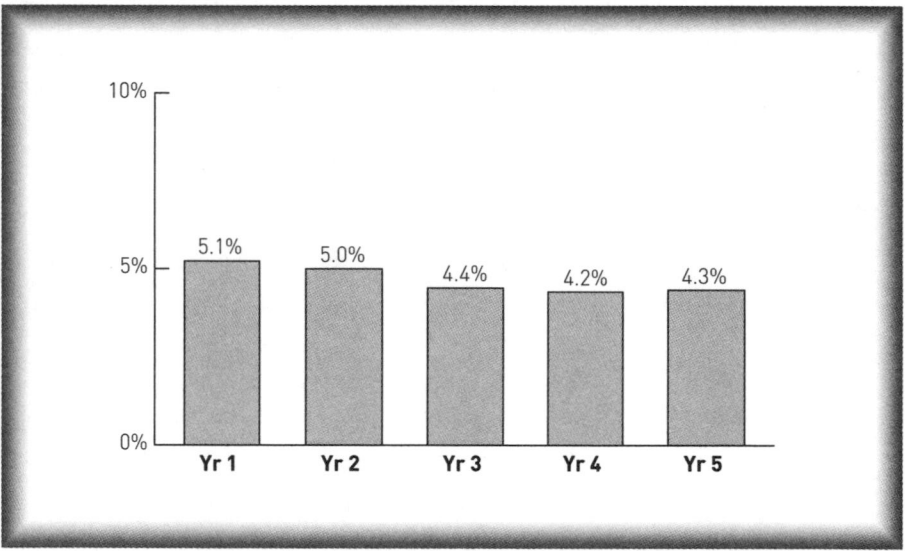

Figure 9.6 Wingate's administration costs as a percentage of sales (years 1–5)

This reduction explains why the return on sales has not fallen as dramatically as the gross margin: savings have been made in administra-

tion. Obviously, there is a limit to the amount by which administration costs can be reduced, so the outlook for return on sales and thus return on capital could be even worse than the historic trends suggest.

One interesting thing about these administration costs is the sudden drop in year three. Do you know of anything that happened around then, Tom?

I believe that was when we moved all the office staff into the new building.

And I presume the old building was rented and the new one is owned by the company?

Yes.

So in fact all that has happened from an accounting point of view is that Wingate has reduced its operating expenses because it is no longer paying rent, but the capital employed in the business will have gone up as a result of building new offices. The effect of this is to improve ROS, but decrease capital productivity. The net impact on the key measure, ROCE, will probably be very small; for all we know, it could have got worse, not better. In other words, this reduction in administration costs is actually nothing to get excited about.

Employee productivity

As well as the expenses itemised on the P&L, the notes to the accounts also provide information which can help to explain why operating profits are behaving as they are.

Note 4 [page 283] shows the number of employees in different categories. From this we can calculate the **sales per employee**. As a general rule, we would expect that, in a well-managed company, sales per employee would be rising faster than sales due to improvements in efficiency and technological innovation. We can also calculate this ratio for each of the different types of employee itemised.

A comparison of these ratios with competitors' can be particularly revealing about efficiency and productivity gains in different companies.

Capital ratios

To understand why the capital productivity has declined we need to look at the constituents of capital employed and understand how they have been behaving.

Fixed asset productivity

As we have seen before, total capital employed is made up of fixed assets and working capital. We can thus look at how 'productive' these two groups of capital have been. For example, to calculate **fixed asset productivity** we simply divide sales by the fixed assets (at the end of the year):

$$
\begin{aligned}
\textbf{Fixed asset productivity} \;&=\; \textbf{Sales / Fixed assets} \\
&=\; 10{,}437 \,/\, 5{,}326 \\
&=\; 2.0
\end{aligned}
$$

This says that Wingate got £2 of sales out of each £1 of fixed assets. The following graph [Figure 9.7] shows how this has changed over the five years.

As with capital productivity, we would like fixed asset productivity to be as high as possible. In Wingate's case, it has declined from 2.5 to 2.0, a drop of 20 per cent. As you can see, it appears to have risen over the last year from 1.9 to 2.0. Whether this is a reversal of the trend remains to be seen – it could be just a temporary blip.

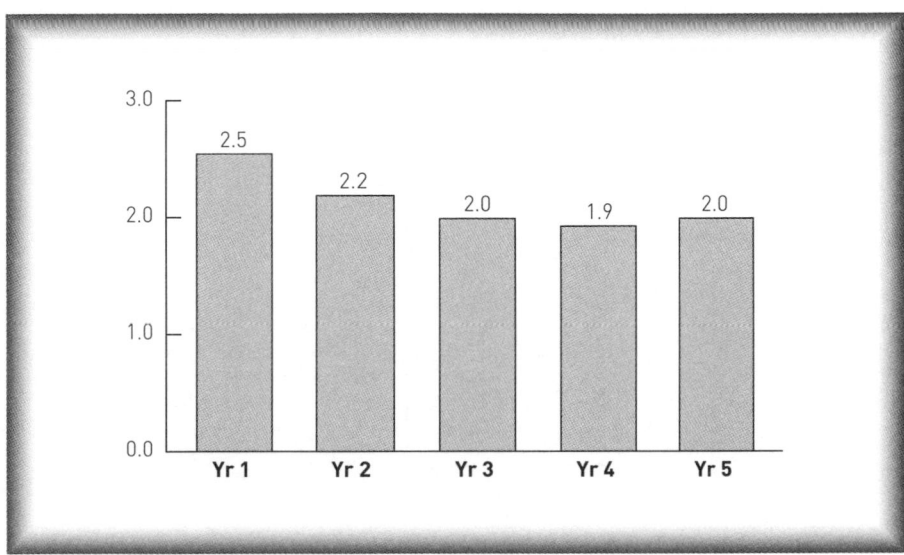

Figure 9.7 Wingate's fixed asset productivity (years 1–5)

We could, of course, now look at how the productivities of the individual fixed asset categories have changed, which may provide further insight.

Working capital productivity

We calculate this exactly as we did fixed asset productivity (i.e. sales divided by working capital). The five-year picture is as follows [Figure 9.8].

Working capital productivity has declined from 11.8 to 6.2, which is a fall in productivity of 47.5 per cent.

That's appalling isn't it? No wonder ROCE has fallen.

Well, let's just think about that for a second, Tom. If you owned £10,000 worth of shares in one company and £100 worth of shares in another, you would be much more concerned if the first shares fell by 10 per cent (since you would have lost £1,000) than you would if the second fell by 50 per cent (since you would have only lost £50).

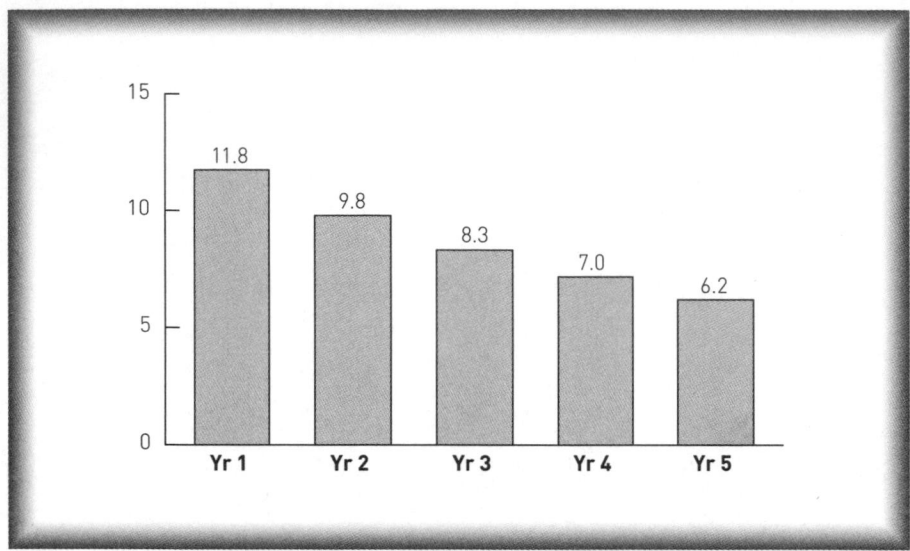

Figure 9.8 Wingate's working capital productivity (years 1–5)

The point I'm making is that you have to look at the relative scale of things. Working capital is only a small part of Wingate's capital employed; the bulk is fixed assets. We are still getting £6.20 of sales for every pound of working capital, whereas we only get £2 of sales for every pound of fixed assets.

Presumably, if you can avoid paying your creditors for a long time and persuade your debtors to pay you quickly, you can get an incredibly high working capital productivity?

You can, but remember what I said about profit versus cash flow. To get a high working capital productivity, you will probably have to give your customers a discount for early payment and you will have to pay your suppliers more to take deferred payment. As a result, you would be cutting your profit margins.

There is a more important point here as well. Let's assume you do get your working capital down to a very low level (and therefore its productivity is very high). If, suddenly, some of your customers decided not to pay quickly, you might find yourself without any cash coming in to pay your suppliers. If you are already taking a long time to pay them, they could get very impatient very quickly. If you have no cash in the bank and/or overdraft facility available from a bank, this could be a real problem.

Having said all that, this level of decline in working capital productivity is pretty dreadful. Let's see what has been going on by looking at the productivity of some of the individual constituents of working capital.

Trade debtor productivity, trade debtor days

We calculate sales for every pound of trade debtors exactly as we did for the other capital ratios. What we get is shown in Figure 9.9.

Analysts tend to look at this ratio another way. We know what Wingate's sales were for the year. If we assume these sales were spread

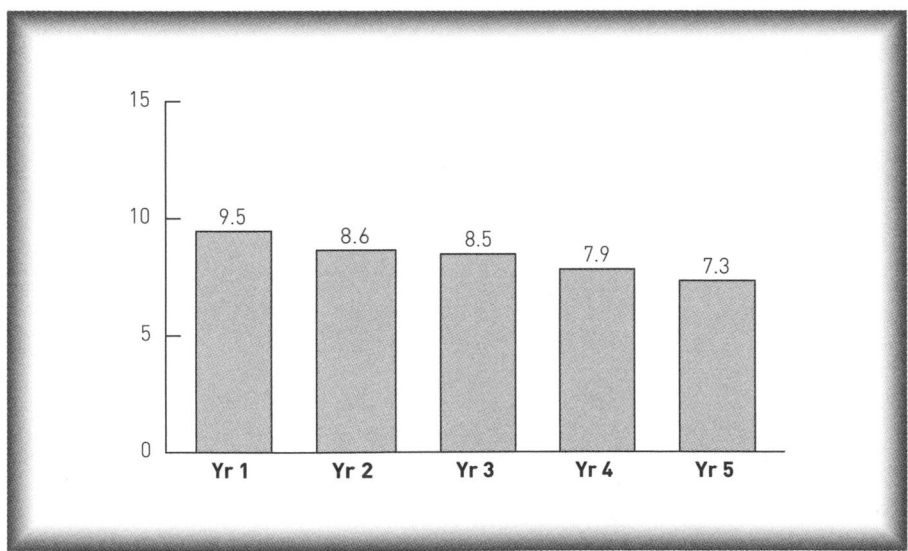

Figure 9.9 Wingate's trade debtor productivity (years 1–5)

evenly throughout the year, then we can calculate what the average daily sales were. Knowing what customers owed Wingate at the year end, we can say how many days' worth of sales that represents. Hence for year five:

$$
\begin{aligned}
\textbf{Daily sales} \quad &= \quad \textbf{Annual sales / Days in a year} \\
&= \quad 10{,}437 \,/\, 365 \\
&= \quad \pounds 28.6k \\[1em]
\textbf{Trade debtor days} \quad &= \quad \textbf{Trade debtors / Daily sales} \\
&= \quad 1{,}250 \,/\, 28.6 \\
&= \quad 44 \text{ days}
\end{aligned}
$$

This suggests that Wingate is waiting on average 44 days before being paid.

Where do you get the figure 1,250 from? Wingate's trade debtors at the end of year five were £1,437k.

You have to remember that the trade debtors figure will include VAT, whereas the sales figure will not. I have assumed that the VAT rate is 15 per cent and have therefore divided the £1,437k figure by 1.15 to get the trade debtors figure excluding VAT.

Over the five-year period, we can see that Wingate has been giving its customers longer and longer to pay [Figure 9.10].

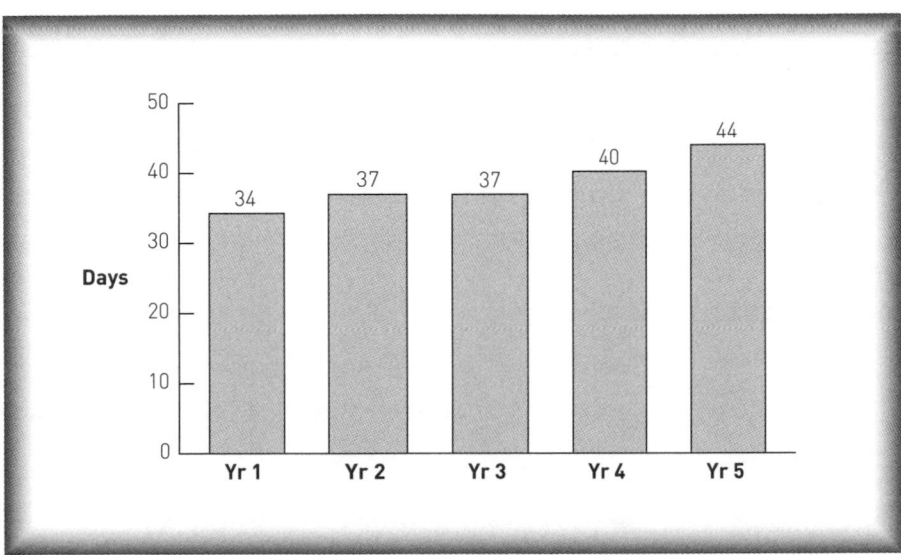

Figure 9.10 Wingate's trade debtor days (years 1–5)

Trade creditor productivity

The trade creditor productivity (again calculated as sales divided by trade creditors) has risen over the five-year period [Figure 9.11].

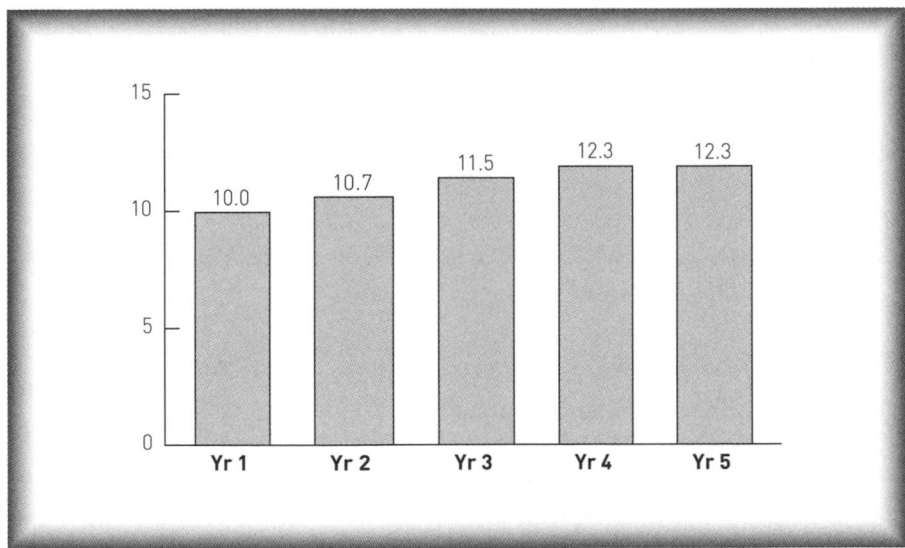

Figure 9.11 Wingate's trade creditor productivity (years 1–5)

This is not good, however, from the point of view of getting a high return on capital. Creditors reduce working capital. Hence we want creditor productivity to be as low as possible. This graph suggests that Wingate has been paying creditors more quickly than it used to. This is probably to get better prices but it may be that the finance department just hasn't been trying hard enough!

Stock productivity, stock days

Let's see how Wingate has been managing its stock over the last five years by looking at stock productivity (sales divided by stock) [Figure 9.12].

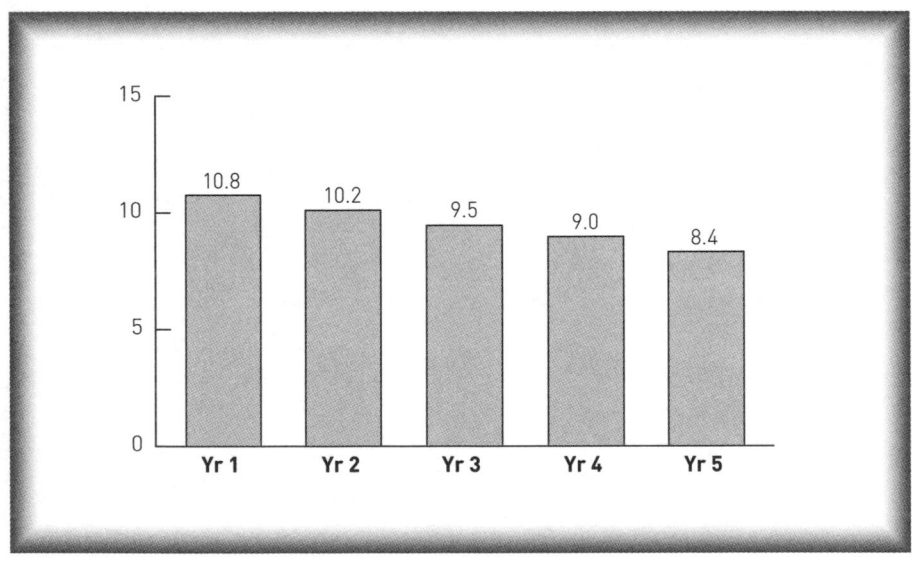

Figure 9.12 Wingate's stock productivity (years 1–5)

Sales per pound of stock have been declining, contributing to the reduction in working capital productivity.

As we did with debtors, we can determine the number of days worth of finished stock that Wingate has in its warehouse. We know that the amount of stock sold each day is simply the cost of goods sold for the year divided by the number of days in a year.

The number of days of finished goods is then easily calculated:

Daily stock sales	=	**Annual COGS / Days in a year**
	=	8,078 / 365
	=	£21.1k
Finished stock days	=	**Finished stock/Daily stock sales**
	=	862/22.1
	=	39 days

As you can see from my next graph, the number of days' worth of finished stock has been rising steadily over the last five years [Figure 9.13].

All in all, Wingate has not been managing its working capital at all. Let's now pull it all together and summarise what we have found out about Wingate.

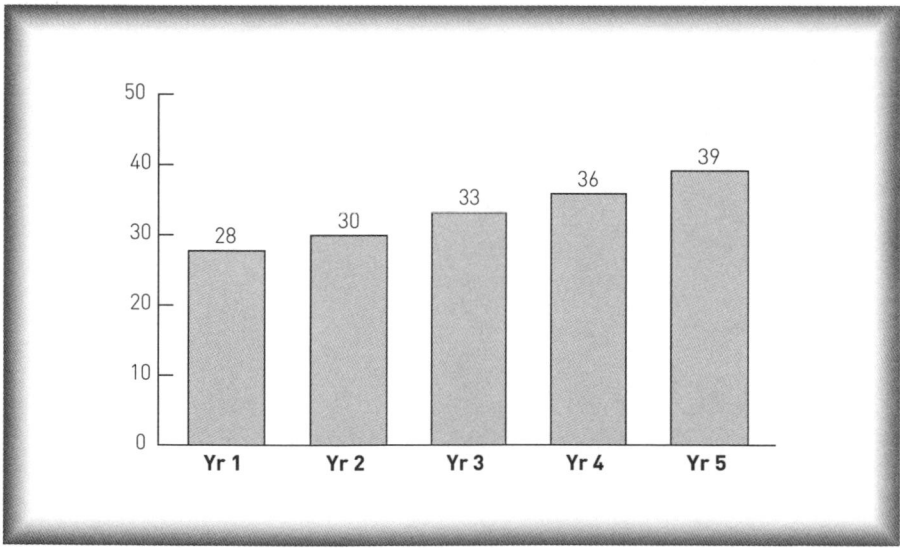

Figure 9.13 Wingate's finished stock days (years 1–5)

SUMMARY

- Wingate's return on capital employed, which is the key performance measure of the enterprise, has been declining dramatically since the new management took charge – although operating profit has been growing, capital employed has been growing faster.

- The decline in ROCE can be explained by a decline in both return on sales and capital productivity.

- The fall in ROS is due to a steady decline in gross margin, probably caused by the management's price-cutting policy. The gross margin decline has been offset to some extent by a reduction in administration costs (only made possible, however, by investing in new buildings).

- Capital productivity has fallen because both fixed assets and working capital are growing faster than sales.

- The disproportionate need for additional working capital is because the company is not collecting its debts from customers as quickly, is holding more stock than it used to and is paying its suppliers sooner.

Now we need to look at the funding structure and see how that affects our views of the company. What I'm going to do first is show you how we summarise the funding structure in a simple ratio.

10

Analysis of the funding structure

- The funding structure ratios
- Lenders' perspective
- Gearing
- Shareholders' perspective
- Liquidity
- Summary

We have looked at Wingate's underlying business and discovered that it is a much less attractive picture than the management would have you believe, Tom. Now we need to look at the funding structure and see how that affects our views of the company. What I am going to do first is show you how we summarise the funding structure in a simple ratio. We will then look at the implications of that structure from the different points of view of the lenders (i.e. the banks) and the shareholders.

The funding structure ratios

When we rearranged Wingate's balance sheet in session 7, we established that the funding for the business was a combination of tax payable, debt and equity [Table 10.1].

The total amount of funding is, as it has to be, the same as the capital employed in the enterprise. We have seen how to calculate the return on this capital. What we are interested in now is the way the funding is made up, i.e. what proportion of the funding comes from each of the different sources.

WINGATE FOODS PLC

Funding structure

		£'000
Taxation		202
Net debt		
Cash	(15)	
Overdraft	893	
Loans	3,000	
	———	
Net debt		3,878
Shareholders' equity		
Dividends payable	154	
Share capital	50	
Share premium	275	
Retained profit	2,446	
	———	
Total shareholders' equity		2,925
		———
Net funding		7,005

Table 10.1 Wingate's funding structure

In practice, tax payable is usually very small in comparison with debt and equity. This is certainly true of Wingate, as you can see from Table 10.1 which shows tax payable to be £202k against debt of £3,878k and equity of £2,925k. Tax only complicates the situation and, since it is so small, we just ignore it and concentrate on the debt and the equity.

The debt to total funding ratio

Ignoring tax payable, the total funding of a business is the sum of the debt and the equity. The **debt to total funding ratio** is the debt divided

by the total funding, i.e. it shows what percentage of the total funding is debt:

> **Debt to total funding = Debt / Total funding**
> = 3,878 / (3,878 + 2,925)
> = 57.0%

I'll come on to the implications of this figure later, but to give you an idea of what is normal:

- Anything over 50 per cent is considered pretty high.

- The average for the top 100 companies in Britain is around 25 per cent.

The debt to equity ratio (or 'gearing')

The debt to total funding ratio shows you at a glance how much of a business is funded by debt and, by deduction, how much by equity. Many people prefer, however, to summarise the funding structure in a slightly different way. They divide the debt by the equity and express it as a percentage. This ratio, known as the **debt to equity ratio** or **gearing**, shows how large the debt is relative to the equity.

> **Debt to equity = Debt / Equity**
> = 3,878 / 2,925
> = 133%

This tells us that Wingate's debt is 1.33 times bigger than its equity. The two benchmark figures of 25 per cent and 50 per cent, which I just gave you for debt to total funding, are the equivalent of debt to equity ratios of 33 per cent and 100 per cent respectively.

The debt to equity ratio is probably the more common of the two ratios. Personally, I find the debt to total funding ratio much easier to interpret quickly, so I have used it in my analysis of Wingate.

Wingate's five-year debt to total funding ratio

Over the last five years, Wingate has increased the amount of debt in its funding structure markedly [Figure 10.1].

Back in year one it was at a fairly conservative level; currently it is over the 50 per cent threshold at which people start to look at the company very carefully. Let's now see why people care about this ratio; we'll start by looking at it from the perspective of lenders (i.e. the banks).

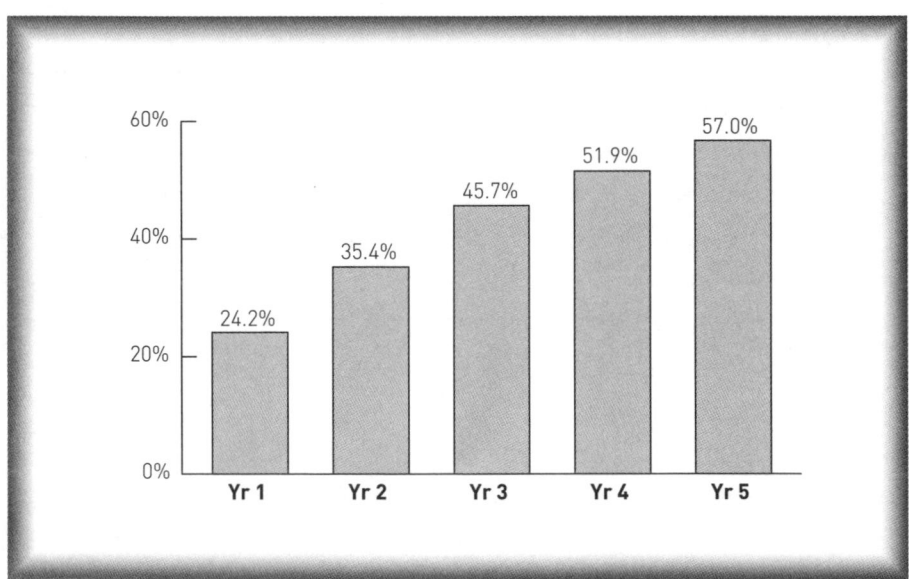

Figure 10.1 Wingate's debt to total funding ratio (years 1–5)

Lenders' perspective

Security of debt

When a bank lends money to a company, it is making an investment. People and companies put their spare cash into current accounts, deposit accounts, etc. at their banks. The banks then lend this cash to other people and companies who need it. The banks make a profit by paying a lower interest rate to the people depositing their money than they charge to the people who borrow from them.

This sounds like money for old rope and it is, provided that everyone who borrows money from the bank repays it eventually. The banks only make a few percentage points out of each pound they lend. By the time they have paid all their costs, their profit is a fraction of a percentage point of the money they lend. If, therefore, someone doesn't repay the loan, it wipes out all the profit on hundreds of their other loans.

Because of this, banks always look for some **security** – anything that gives them confidence that they will get their money back.

As I mentioned when we were looking at Wingate's accounts in detail [session 6], most companies with overdrafts or loans will have given the bank a charge over their assets. This means that if the company goes bust, the bank has first right to sell the assets and take the cash.

The proceeds from selling assets will not always be enough to cover the bank's debt if a large percentage of the funding structure is debt. Hence the debt to total funding ratio gives an idea of the bank's risk.

Surely the assets must always be worth more than the debt?

Not necessarily, Sarah. Remember the going concern concept. A company might buy an asset which is no use to anyone else in the world and therefore has no resale value. We would still give this asset a value in the company's books, as it is of use in the company's ongoing operations.

On top of that, a bank will only want to sell a company's assets when the company is effectively bust. In that situation, even assets that are of use to other people will be hard to sell for their full value.

But presumably some of the assets, like debtors, you would get most of their book value for, and others, like specialised machinery, you would get next to nothing for?

Of course. In practice, bankers do much more detailed checks and analyses to ensure their loans are secure, but the debt to total funding ratio does give an instant idea of the position.

Wingate's bankers were probably told by the company's management that by investing in fixed assets and expanding sales rapidly, the company could reduce its unit costs and make bumper profits. If I were a banker, after watching the ROCE decline for four years and the debt to total funding ratio rise, I would be getting extremely sceptical by now. I would be looking for some convincing evidence that the company's cash flow and return on capital were going to turn round very soon.

Interest cover

Lenders are concerned at the security of their debt and rightly so. Good bankers, however, do not make loans in the expectation that they will have to sell the company's assets to get their money back. Their hope and expectation is that the company will pay the interest on the debt for as long as required, and then repay the principal.

One of the other key measures used by lenders is interest cover. This is calculated by dividing operating profit by the interest payable:

Interest cover = Operating profit / Interest payable
= 929 / 299
= 3.1

Operating profits are applied first to paying interest on the debt. This ratio shows literally that Wingate could pay 3.1 times as much interest as it has to. What a banker would think of this depends on the economic climate at the time. In the mid-1980s, banks were lending money in situations where their interest cover was as low as 1.5 times. In the recession that followed, banks were demanding interest cover of greater than five times!

Gearing

We can now see why the funding structure is important to lenders. We have also seen that the bankers might be getting a little worried by Wingate's situation. Before looking at the shareholders' perspective, you need to understand the concept of **gearing** and its implications. A while ago, I told you that gearing was another word for the debt to equity ratio, which it is. 'Gearing' is also used more generally to describe the concept of borrowing money to add to your own money to make an investment. You will also hear the American word 'leverage' used to mean the same thing.

Let's see how this can affect your wealth by looking at a simple example. Assume you have been given an opportunity to invest in some rare stamps. The dealer has told you that they will probably go up in value by 15 per cent during the year. You know, however, that there is a risk that they will only go up by 5 per cent. You decide to take the risk.

The dealer has £500 worth of the stamps available, but you have only £100 to spare. Let's look at several different scenarios.

Scenario one – no debt

Assume for our first scenario that you decide just to invest the £100 you have. We will call this £100 your 'equity'.

If things go well, the stamps will go up in value to £115 at the end of the year. The profit on your equity will be £15, which is a return of 15 per cent on your investment.

If things go badly, your profit will only be £5, which is a 5 per cent return.

Scenario two – some debt

Let's assume instead that you decide to borrow an additional £100 from the bank to enable you to buy £200 worth of the stamps. The interest you will have to pay on the loan is 10 per cent per annum. Now the total investment is made up of your equity of £100 and debt of £100.

If things go well, the profit on the total investment is now £30. Out of this profit, however, you have to pay the bank's interest, which will be £10. You will be left with £20 profit from your £100 equity, giving you a return of 20 per cent.

If things go badly and the stamps only go up by 5 per cent to £210, the profit on the investment is only £10. You *still* have to pay the bank its £10 interest, which would leave you with nothing.

So could I end up actually losing money?

Let's see.

Scenario three – mostly debt

Assume you borrow £400 from the bank to go with your £100, thereby enabling you to buy all £500 worth of the stamps.

If things go well, the investment will make a profit of £75. Of this profit, £40 will go to the bank as interest on their £400 loan. The balance of the profit will be yours. You will make £35 profit on an investment of £100, which is a return of 35 per cent. If things go badly, though, the investment will only make £25 profit. Unfortunately, you will still owe the bank £40 interest, so you will have to find the extra £15 to pay them. You have made a loss of £15 on your £100 investment, which is a return of minus 15 per cent.

This is the situation in which many people during the recession of the early 1990s found themselves with regard to their homes. They put some of their own money towards buying their house. This is what building societies euphemistically called a 'deposit'. The rest of the money needed to buy the house came as a loan from the building society. In the good times of the early to middle 1980s, people could borrow the majority of the price of their houses, knowing that house prices would rise and they could sell the house, pay off the building society and pocket a nice profit.

In the recession, many houses fell in value so that, if the owners sold the house, they ended up owing the building society more than they got for the house, i.e. they had 'negative equity'. It's exactly the same principle.

Risk and return

Let's just summarise the return you would have made in each of the different scenarios:

		If the market went ...	
		Well	Badly
Increase in value of assets		15%	5%
Return on your investment			
Scenario one	– No debt	15%	5%
Scenario two	– Some debt	20%	0%
Scenario three	– Lots of debt	35%	–15%

What this shows is that if you do not take out any debt at all, your return will match that of the underlying asset. As soon as you introduce some debt, then the returns become **geared**. The more debt you include, the higher the return you will make in the good times, but the lower the return you will make in the bad times. In other words, you have to take a greater risk to get a greater return.

How do you define the good times versus the bad times?

Simple. Provided the underlying asset gives a return greater than the interest on the debt, then gearing will lead to higher returns for the equity. In our example, provided the underlying asset provides a return of more than 10 per cent, then you would make a better return if you had some gearing.

So how does all this apply to companies?

Think of the stamps as being the enterprise. They are the operating assets, which may or may not make a good profit. The money that you put towards buying the stamps is equivalent to the equity in a company's funding structure; the money that the bank put towards buying the stamps is the debt in the company's funding structure.

Presumably, the more geared you are, the more a change in interest rates affects you?

Yes, it works in the same way as a change in the return of the enterprise. Unfortunately, a rise in interest rates is often accompanied by worse performance in the enterprise, so you get a 'double-whammy' effect. Naturally, you benefit when interest rates go down.

Shareholders' perspective

Debt to total funding ratio

As we have just seen, gearing affects the risk of and potential returns to shareholders. Shareholders ought, therefore, to control the level of debt a company takes on but, in practice, the management tends to decide. The shareholders can, of course, remove the management of a company if they don't like what they see.

Given that Wingate's debt to total funding ratio has risen from 24 per cent to 57 per cent, the shareholders' risk has risen considerably.

Return on equity

So Wingate's shareholders have a much more risky company than five years ago. What about the return they are getting?

We know from our analysis of the enterprise that the return on capital employed of the enterprise has fallen to around 13 per cent. But that is the return on the total funding. Shareholders, ultimately, are interested in the return on the money they have invested, i.e. the **return on equity** (known as **ROE**). We calculated this earlier when we were looking at the investment in stamps.

We can do the same calculation for Wingate. We know what the equity is – we can read it off Table 10.1. The return is the profit after paying the interest on the loans, i.e. profit before tax.

> **Return on equity = Profit before tax / Equity**
> = 630 / 2,925
> = 21.5%

So you're using the equity at the end of the year, as you did for the ROCE?

Yes. As with ROCE, you could use the equity at the start of the year if you wanted to – just make sure you are consistent.

Why are you using the profit before tax? Surely the actual profit to the share-holders is the profit for the year, i.e. profit after tax and extraordinary items?

Arguably, but so far we have been calculating returns before tax. For example, we talked about getting 5 per cent per annum before tax on a deposit account and our calculation of return on capital employed for the enterprise did not take account of tax. In a minute we are going to compare the return on capital employed with the return on equity and obviously they must be calculated on the same basis.

You will, I admit, often see return on equity calculated using profit after tax or profit for the year. This does have one benefit, which is that it takes into account the company's ability to reduce the tax it pays, and some companies do manage to pay consistently less tax than others. In general, though, I think you will find that using profit before tax is more helpful.

I have the feeling that, if I were trying to do this calculation for a company with more complex accounts, it wouldn't be so easy. What if, for example, I wanted to calculate the return on equity for a company that had preference shares, minority interests, etc.?

The secret when calculating any ratio like return on equity is to make sure the elements of the ratio are *matched*. For example, when calculating return on equity for Wingate, we wouldn't use operating profit as the return figure because that is not the profit attributable to the equity. Some of the operating profit is attributable to the lenders. Profit before tax, however, is *all* attributable to the equity (even though they will have to pay some tax on it).

Let's now see how Wingate's ROE has changed over the last five years [Figure 10.2].

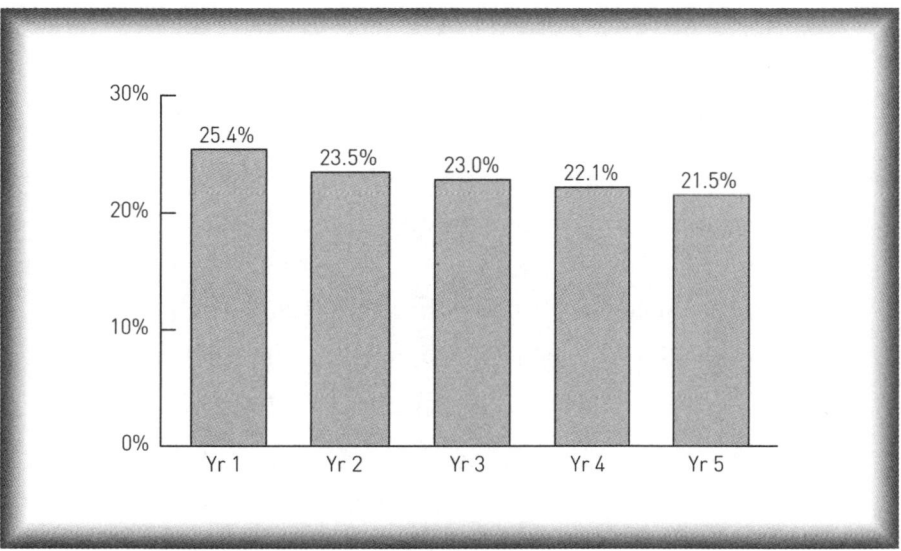

Figure 10.2 Wingate's return on equity (years 1–5)

There are two things to notice about this chart:

- The ROE is consistently higher than the ROCE [page 172]. This is because the return on the enterprise is greater than the interest rate Wingate is paying. In other words, gearing has improved the returns to the shareholders.

- The ROE is declining, but not as fast as the ROCE. This is simply because the company is increasing the gearing of the company so quickly. The decline in the ROCE is being offset by the positive impact on ROE that the gearing is having.

Naturally, this trend cannot continue. Ultimately, the return on capital employed would fall below the bank interest rates and the company would be in serious trouble.

Average interest rate

Companies whose shares are quoted on the Stock Exchange have to tell you what their average interest rates were during the year. Private companies don't have to. You can make a guess, however, just by knowing what base rates were at the time and adding a few percentage points.

You can also get a very crude estimate from the accounts by taking the interest paid during the year and dividing it by the average debt at the start and end of the year. You have to be careful about this calculation as companies' overdrafts can vary substantially during a year, depending on the seasonality of the business, so the result you will get from this calculation depends on the balance sheet date.

There is probably not much seasonality in Wingate's business as it is a food company, so let's do the calculation anyway. Wingate's debt was £2,843k at the start of year five and £3,878k at the end. The average debt is therefore £3,361k.

Average interest rate = Interest / Average debt
$$= 299 / 3,361$$
$$= 8.9\%$$

If we look at Wingate's average interest rate over the last five years [Figure 10.3], you can see why, despite large rises in debt, Wingate has been able to report ever-increasing profit before tax: quite simply, the interest rate has gone in its favour.

Let's see what Wingate's profit before tax in year five would be if the average interest rate were still 13.2 per cent. The extra interest Wingate would have had to pay is £3,361 × (13.2 – 8.9) per cent which is £145k

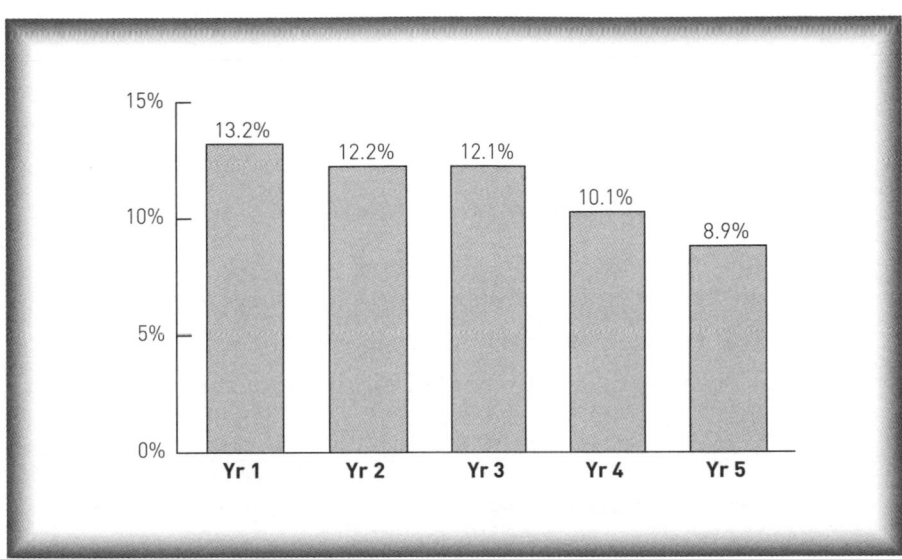

Figure 10.3 Wingate's average interest rate (years 1–5)

of extra interest. This reduces profit before tax in year five from £630k to £485k, only just more than Wingate made back in year one.

Dividend cover, payout ratio

Although ROE measures the return to shareholders for having invested their money in a company over the last year, they do not actually get all this return out of the company in the form of cash. Remember that profit is not cash. The company is probably still waiting to collect cash from debtors and has manufactured more stock for next year, etc. Some of the profit, however, is paid out in the form of dividends.

Some shareholders rely upon these dividends as a key source of income and they are naturally interested to know how safe the dividends are. One measure of this is **dividend cover**, which is calculated as profit for the year divided by the dividend:

> **Dividend cover = Profit for the year / Dividend**
> = 422 / 154
> = 2.7

You will sometimes find people using a measure called the **payout ratio**. This is simply the inverse of dividend cover expressed as a percentage. It shows what percentage of the profit for the year is paid out as dividends:

> **Payout ratio = Dividend / Profit for the year**
> = 154 / 422
> = 37%

Let's now look at Wingate's dividend cover over the last five years [Figure 10.4].

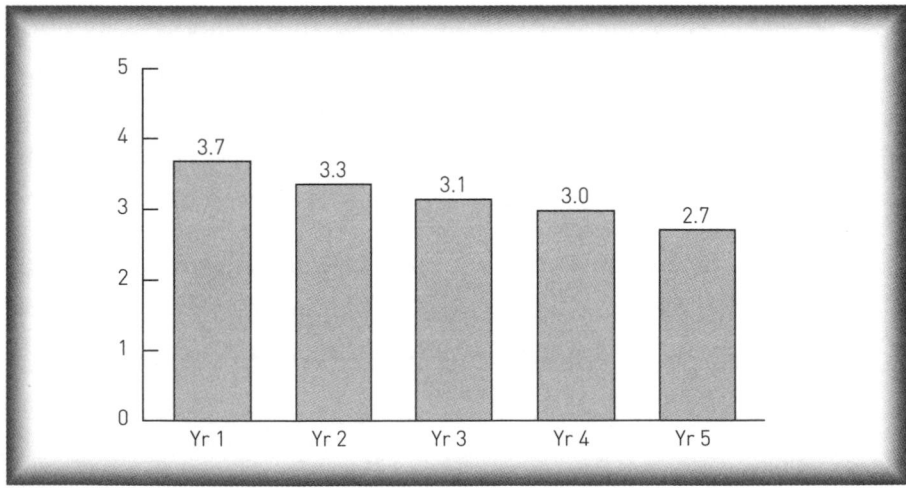

Figure 10.4 Wingate's dividend cover (years 1–5)

As you can see, it has been falling quite markedly. This explains why the shareholders are happy. Although the profit attributable to shareholders has not been growing very fast, the dividends have been doing so as a result of paying out an ever-increasing percentage of the profits. Obviously this is not sustainable in the long run.

Liquidity

You summed up the financial objectives of a company very neatly earlier, Sarah. What you said was:

> "A company's main objective is to maximise the return it provides on the money invested, based on an appropriate trade-off between the short- and long-term perspectives, while ensuring that the business remains liquid."

We have been analysing the returns that Wingate has been providing, both on the total capital employed in the business (ROCE) and on the shareholders' capital (ROE).

We have not paid much attention to liquidity so far. As you will remember, liquidity is the ability of a company to pay its debts as they fall due. Analysing a company's liquidity is extremely difficult. There is no single parameter that tells us very much.

There are two ratios which are commonly used as measures of liquidity which I will mention briefly but they are by no means perfect.

Current ratio

The **current ratio** is calculated by dividing the current assets by the current liabilities. The logic behind this is that the current assets should all be convertible into cash within one year, and the current liabilities are what you have to pay within one year. Provided your current

assets are greater than your current liabilities, you should not have a liquidity problem.

We can calculate the current ratio for Wingate very easily:

$$
\begin{aligned}
\textbf{Current ratio} &= \textbf{Current assets / Current liabilities} \\
&= 2{,}817 \,/\, 2{,}372 \\
&= 1.2
\end{aligned}
$$

In other words, Wingate's current assets are 1.2 times greater than its current liabilities. Typically, analysts look for this ratio to be greater than 2.0 to give a good margin of safety.

What is wrong with the current ratio as a measure of liquidity?

The major problem is that liquidity crises tend to have a much shorter time horizon than a year. If you have to pay some bills this week to continue trading, it is no comfort to know that your customers will be paying you in two months' time. The safety implied by a given current ratio figure will depend on the nature of a company's business.

You can always look at the trend in a company's current ratio, but you have to be very careful about companies which find ways to redefine short-term liabilities as long-term liabilities, thereby improving their current ratios. Switching between overdrafts and loans is one easy way to do this.

Quick ratio

The **quick ratio** is identical to the current ratio except that stock is not included in the current assets, on the basis that stock can be hard to sell. All the other assets (principally debtors and cash) are 'quick'.

The quick ratio suffers from exactly the same problems as the current ratio.

So how do you assess liquidity?

Ideally, you make week-by-week or month-by-month forecasts of exactly what bills are going to have to be paid when, and what customers are going to pay when, etc.

This, of course, is impossible from outside the company. If you only have the annual reports, I recommend looking at the cash flow statement.

The cash flow statement

From the cash flow statement [pages 280–281] you can see quite clearly where cash has been coming from and going to.

- The first section shows us what cash is being generated by the operating activities before any further investment in fixed assets. On the face of it, this is not too bad, being nearly £1m in year 5.

- Under the heading 'Capital expenditure' we can see the expenditure on fixed assets, which for Wingate is substantially more than the cash coming out of the operating activities.

The following graph [Figure 10.5] shows the cash flow of the enterprise over the last five years. The shaded bars show the cash flow before taking account of the cash spent on new fixed assets. The hatched bars show the cash flow after spending on fixed assets.

As you can see, net cash flow from the enterprise ('operating cash flow') has been consistently negative and there is no sign of the cash flow reversing and the enterprise actually increasing the amount of cash in the business. Even if it could reach a situation where the cash generated from operations was equal to the capital expenditure requirement ('cash neutral' as they say), there's still nearly £300,000 of interest, dividends and tax to pay.

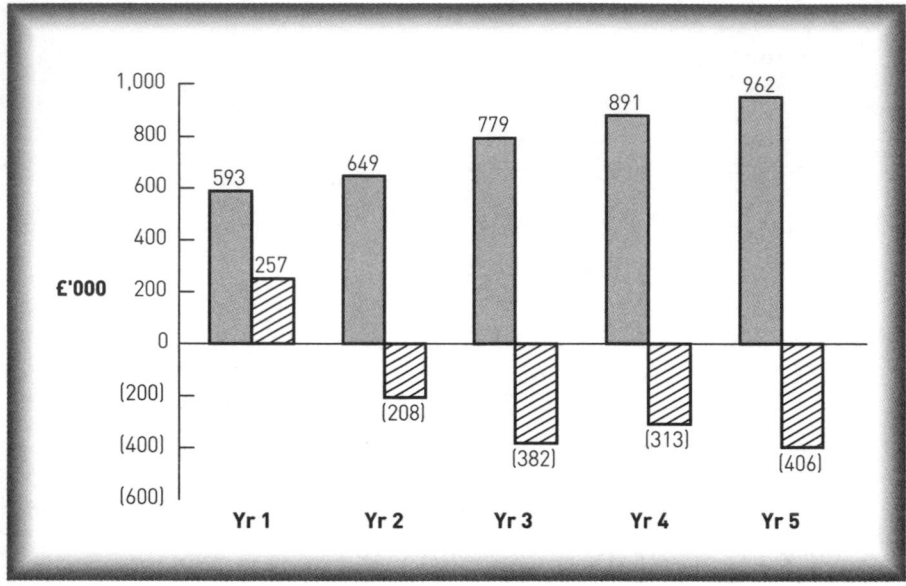

Figure 10.5 Cash flow from Wingate's enterprise (years 1–5)

As a result, it is clear that the company will have to either stop spending on fixed assets or raise more money. Given a debt to total funding ratio of 57 per cent, it seems likely that the banks will be disinclined to provide further funds. I would therefore anticipate an imminent cash crisis at Wingate, unless some radical action is taken.

SUMMARY

- Wingate's gearing (as measured by the debt to equity and debt to total funding ratios) has been rising rapidly and is now well above average levels.

- This means that the lenders' security has diminished and they are unlikely to lend further funds.

- The rise in gearing has also affected the shareholders' position:
  - Their return (as measured by ROE) has not fallen as fast as it would otherwise have done.
  - Their risk has risen substantially, however.

- Without a decline in interest rates, Wingate's profit before tax would barely have risen over the last four years.

- Dividends are only growing strongly because the company is paying out an ever-increasing proportion of its profits.

- The trend in the cash flow of the enterprise suggests that Wingate will have to either raise further funds or make a dramatic change in its strategy.

What I'm going to say really only applies to listed shares, i.e. shares whose prices are quoted every day on a stock exchange and which anyone can buy through a stockbroker.

Valuation of companies

- Book value vs market value
- Valuation techniques
- Summary

So far we have talked about how to construct, interpret and analyse company accounts. Someone like you, Tom, who is thinking of buying shares in a company is really interested in the value of those shares (which is what most people mean when they talk about the value of a 'company').

What I am going to say really only applies to listed shares, i.e. shares whose prices are quoted every day on a stock exchange and which anyone can buy through a stockbroker. Unlisted companies can be valued using the same principles but, in practice, there are many other factors that have to be taken into account.

I will start by explaining why book value and market value of shares are usually different and then I will describe briefly the most common methods of valuation.

Book value vs market value

Book value

Book value is simply the value that an item has on the balance sheet (i.e. 'in the books'). We know that the book value of the shares of a company is the value of the equity, which is the difference between the assets and the liabilities. At the end of year five, Wingate's equity, and therefore the book value of the shares, was £2,925k (including the dividends payable).

If you own just a few shares in the company, this figure does not tell you very much, so we can express it on a 'per share' basis. We know that Wingate has one million shares in issue, all of which have an equal right to the net assets, so the book value per share is as follows:

BV per share = **BV / Number of shares**
= 2,925k / 1m
= £2.93 per share

Market value

The balance sheet tells us what our shares are worth in the eyes of the accountants. The fact is, though, that we live in a market economy, where things are worth what someone will pay for them, not what anyone's 'books' say they are worth. Some companies are worth less than their book value, but most are worth more.

Why would anyone pay more than book value?

There are two possible reasons:

- It may simply be that the market value of one of the assets of the company is much higher than the book value. The most common example of this is land and buildings. If you knew a company had an asset that was worth much more than its value in the books, you might be prepared to pay more than book value for the company so you could sell off the assets and pocket a nice profit.

- In general, though, people don't invest in a company in order to wind it up. They invest in a company because they believe it will provide a good return on the investment. If they can pay more than book

value for the shares and still get a good return on their money, then it makes sense to do so.

Let's take Wingate back in year one as an example. In those days, the company was making a good return on capital employed with a reasonable level of gearing, resulting in a good return to the shareholders, as measured by return on equity calculated as follows:

Profit before tax	£470k
Equity	£1,854k
Return on equity	25.4%

An investor looking at the company might have said, 'This is a well-run company in a good market position. I would accept a lower return than 25.4 per cent from such a company; I would accept 22 per cent'.

Such an investor would be saying:

$$22\% = \text{Profit before tax / Equity value}$$
$$= £470k / ?$$

Hence:
$$\text{Equity value} = £470k / 22\%$$
$$= £2,136k$$
$$= 214p \text{ per share}$$

The investor would therefore be prepared to pay up to 214p per share, which compares with the book value per share at the time of 185p.

Naturally, different investors and analysts will have different opinions on what return is acceptable from a company and therefore arrive at different valuations. Bear in mind as well that the returns we can calculate from the accounts are what has happened in the past. When we value a company we are, implicitly or explicitly, predicting the future, which results in even greater variation in different people's valuations.

Valuation techniques

There are many different techniques used to value companies. Unfortunately, since the value of a company depends on future events, none of these techniques is perfect. The techniques vary from simple ones, which rely on the calculation of a single parameter, to extremely complex ones, which require quantitative analysis of risk and the forecasting of a company's performance for the next ten years.

My personal experience is that the complex techniques are just as bad as the simple ones. It seems that most people have had the same experience, because the simple ones are by far the most common. It may be, of course, that we are all just lazy and have convinced ourselves that the simple way is best! Whatever the reasons, I'm only going to cover the simple ones. If you are interested, there are plenty of books on more complex techniques.

Price earnings ratio (PER or P/E)

The method our hypothetical investor used to decide to pay more than book value for Wingate shares probably seems like a fairly reasonable way to go about putting a value on a company. You assess the company's management, competition, markets, financial structure, etc. and say 'I'm prepared to accept a return of x per cent or more from this company'. The more you pay for the shares, the lower your expected return, so you buy shares up to a price at which the expected return falls to x per cent.

This method is the approach used by the vast majority of analysts and investors, except that they turn the ratio upside down. Instead of dividing the profit by the value of the shares, they divide the value of the shares by the profit. They also use a different profit figure. Instead of using profit before tax, they use profit for the year, which as we saw earlier, is also known as earnings. This ratio thus becomes the **price earnings ratio**.

Let's suppose that the market value of each Wingate share was 500p. The price earnings ratio (based on profit for the year) would be:

P/E ratio   = **Price / Earnings per share**
= 500 / 42.2
= 11.8

But what is this ratio measuring and how do you interpret it?

If you think about it, the ratio is literally measuring the number of years the company would have to earn those profits in order for you to get your money back. So after 11.8 years of earning 42.2p per share, Wingate would have earned 500p per share.

In practice, investors don't think of this ratio in quite these terms. Investors are typically comparing one investment opportunity with many others. They therefore compare the P/E ratios of all the companies and assess them relative to one another. Companies that have good prospects of increasing profits in the future and/or are low-risk tend to be on higher P/E's than companies whose profits are not growing and/or are perceived to be high-risk.

There are some *extremely* crude benchmarks which you may find helpful:

- A company that people believe to be in danger of going bankrupt will be on a P/E of less than 5.

- A company performing poorly would be on a P/E between 5 and 10.

- A company which is doing satisfactorily will be on a P/E of between 10 and 15.

- A company with extremely good prospects will be on a P/E of greater than 15.

Let me stress, though, that these figures vary hugely by industry and economic conditions, so don't rely on them for any important decisions.

It seems a little odd to use a ratio based on historic profit figures to tell you the value of the company when it obviously depends on what is going to happen in the future.

True, but what people actually do is to interpret P/Es in the light of what they know about the expected future performance of a company.

It is quite common also for people to calculate the P/E using their forecasts of the next year's earnings. This is known as a **prospective P/E** or a **forward P/E**. A P/E based on historic profits is often called the historic P/E to make it clear which year's earnings are being used.

Dividend yield

When you invest your money in a deposit account, the bank pays you all your interest. You might decide to leave it in the account and earn interest on the interest the next year, but you can choose to take it out if you want.

Companies tend not to pay out all of the year's profits to their shareholders. Companies that are expanding rapidly need cash to enable them to expand and tend not to pay out much. They have low payout ratios. Other companies, such as utility companies like telephone,

water, gas and electricity, tend not to grow all that fast and thus are able to pay out a higher percentage of their year's profits.

Such companies are often valued using **dividend yield**. This is calculated as the dividends for the year divided by the value of the shares. The average dividend yield of the large companies in Britain is around 3 per cent. Low-growth companies such as utility companies typically pay yields of 5–6 per cent.

Market to book ratio

There is one further simple measure you can use to compare the valuations of companies.

I started this session by explaining why the market value of shares is usually higher than the book value. This leads us to a simple valuation technique, which is to compare the market value with the book value.

What we do is divide the market value of the shares by the book value, which gives us the **market to book ratio**.

Let's assume that someone is prepared to pay 500p per Wingate share. We know that the book value is 293p. Hence we get:

> **Market to book = Market value / Book value**
> = 500 / 293
> = 1.71

We could then compare this with the market to book ratios of other companies and decide whether it seemed reasonable or not. If it seemed low, then we would say the market value should be higher. We might therefore decide to buy some shares. If the ratio seemed too high, we would take that as an indication to sell the shares.

The problem with this method is that there is very large variation in these ratios in different industries and even within the same industry. Investors therefore have difficulty in comparing them. This ratio is useful, however, when valuing companies whose business is just investing in assets (as opposed to operating them). Such businesses include property investment companies and **investment trusts**. Investment trusts are companies that invest in other companies' shares.

SUMMARY

- Accounts tell us the book value of a company's shares.
- The market value of shares is usually different from the book value.
- There are many different methods for valuing companies from the very simple to the extremely complex.
- The most common methods are the price earnings ratio and dividend yield.
- The price earnings ratio can be based on either historic or expected future earnings.
- The market to book ratio can be useful, particularly for valuing companies like investment trusts.

Unfortunately, many listed companies do whatever they can to make themselves look good in the eyes of the analysts and investors.

12

Tricks of the trade

- Self-serving presentation
- Creative accounting
- Why bother?
- Summary

We saw earlier that, based on the management's criteria, Wingate's financial performance looked very satisfactory. We also saw that, based on the right criteria, the reality was very different. I hope that neither of you would consider investing money in Wingate under the current management and strategy.

Exposing the reality was not difficult in Wingate's case, once we knew how to go about it. We were helped by the fact that Wingate's accounts seemed to reflect the facts pretty fairly. Unfortunately, many listed companies do whatever they can to make themselves look good in the eyes of the analysts and investors. The ways that this can be done fall into two categories

- Self-serving presentation

- Creative accounting

By the latter, I'm talking about stretching, or even breaking, the rules of accounting to report figures that suit the company. Over the last ten years, there have been many new rules introduced to stop creative accounting. Unfortunately, as we saw with high profile cases like Enron and Worldcom at the start of the new millennium, the rules haven't always been enough to stop companies and/or individuals.

One of the problems with all the new rules is that company annual reports are now much longer and much more daunting. You should not let this put you off, though. You can still pick out the bits you need to do the analyses we have been talking about.

I know you would like me to present you with a foolproof method of picking shares, Tom, but unfortunately I don't know one. What I *can* do is show you the tricks companies play when preparing their accounts in the hope that you can avoid the worst offenders. I also think that looking at some of the creative accounting will help cement your understanding of accounting.

Self-serving presentation

The chairman's statement / financial review / review of operations

As discussed earlier, there are no rules on what companies can or have to put in these reports. It is really important that you remember that they are written by public relations departments, whose jobs exist to make the company look good. **Read them for what they *don't* say.** Try to get the last two or three years' reports and compare them. Look for things that they used to talk about a lot and now don't mention. This is probably because even the public relations department can't think of anything positive to say about them.

Directors' report

This is often a very dull report, which is all the more reason to read it carefully. Any major events or changes in the company's position during the year or since the year end will be described here. Bad news will be kept as brief as possible and probably be buried in the middle of a paragraph that looks, at a glance, to be about something very innocuous. Check also whether the directors have been selling significant numbers of their shares in the company (or exercising share options and then immediately selling the shares).

But isn't the annual report rather out of date for this kind of information?

Yes, it is. You usually won't get it until several months after the year end. It is, nonetheless, worth looking at as you do want to know if they were selling during the last reported financial year, but you should also check up-to-date information, which you can get from various on-line and off-line sources relatively easily and cheaply; and, of course, you can always ring the company and ask.

Auditors' report

Check the auditors' report briefly to ensure that there are no qualifications. Be very wary of any company with a qualified auditors' report.

Notes to the accounts

In terms of presentation, there is limited latitude in the notes, with one important exception – reported business segments.

Most companies are required to give a breakdown of their sales and profits by segment and/or by geographical region – they can avoid doing this if substantially all of the business is in the same country and in the same business. Check the old annual reports against the current one to see if the country/business segments have been changed. If they have, it may suggest that the company is trying to cover up poor performance in a particular part of the business.

As with the directors' report, remember that bad news will be kept as brief as possible. A particular item I should mention in this context is contingent liability.

If a company has a potential future liability which depends on the outcome of some future event, then it has to disclose this in the notes as a contingent liability. There have been one or two companies in the last decade where contingent liabilities that were declared in the accounts became actual liabilities and resulted in the demise of the companies (and the total loss of the shareholders' money).

So much for presentation, let's now look at how companies actually change the substance of what they are reporting to suit themselves.

Creative accounting

As I said earlier, the rules have been tightened up dramatically. Nonetheless, they still leave room for manoeuvre, particularly if the directors are less than completely committed to telling the whole truth.

Earnings per share remains the key measure that people use to value companies. Most creative accounting is therefore geared towards managing this figure. Since it is pretty hard to play with the number of shares in issue, the focus is on massaging earnings (i.e. profit). We thus have to look at the P&L and see how it can be manipulated.

Before we start, I want to go back to the balance sheet and show you how simple creative accounting is in principle. The key point to remember is that profit for a particular period is not an absolute, pure, right or wrong figure. It depends on a lot of interpretation of rules and judgement. If you remember, we saw how two identical companies could choose different stock valuation policies (e.g. Average vs FIFO) and have different profit figures for the same accounting period. In the long run, of course, their total accumulated profits would be the same. It is the same with all accounting tricks. You can't *create* profit; you can merely move it from one accounting period to another.

Assume for a moment that you have completed your accounting for the current year and therefore have your final balance sheet. You conclude that your profit for the year is not high enough and you want to make it higher. What are your options? Well, let's look at our balance sheet chart :

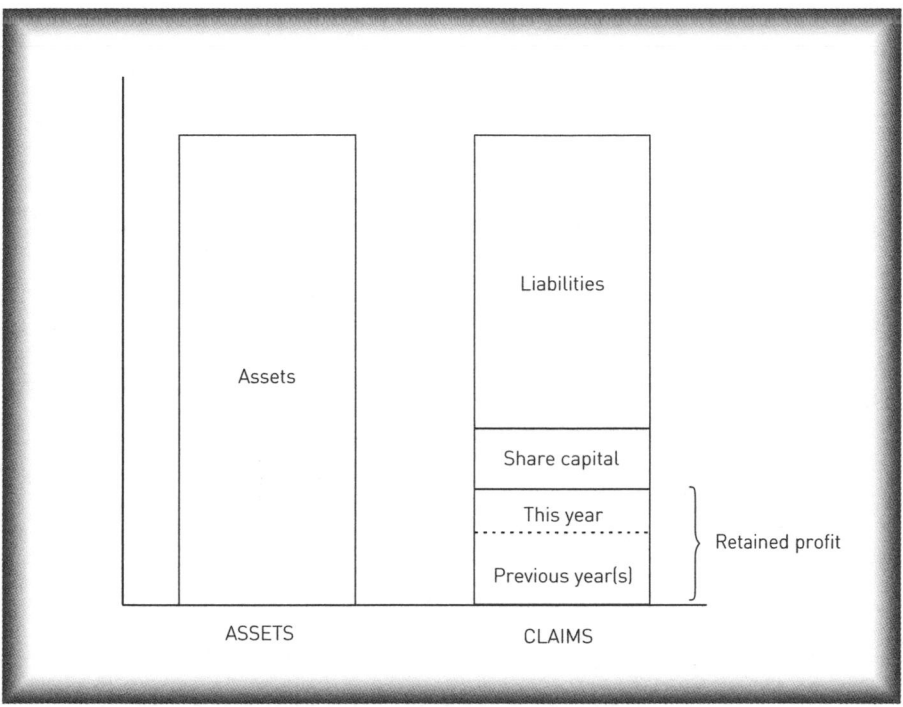

Figure 12.1 Balance sheet chart simplified

Remember that retained profit is your retained profit ever since the company started. You want to make *this year's* retained profit higher. There are several generic ways you might try and do this. Since we know that retained profit is made up of sales (and other forms of income such as interest income) minus expenses, then clearly you need to find more of the former and/or less of the latter. Obviously, therefore, if you can find or create more sales transactions for the year, then you are going to have higher profit for the year. Likewise, if you can find a way not to record in this year's balance sheet an expense transaction, then your profit will be higher.

But you can't just take a transaction out of your balance sheet can you?

You can, but the record of it is always going to be there on your audit trail. Much easier is not to put it in your records in the first place.

Remember that I'm talking about a theoretical situation where you have already finished your balance sheet for the year and prepared it entirely properly and fairly. In practice, companies know well in advance of their year end if they want to play games.

As well as adding or removing transactions, there is another lucrative source of creative accounting possibilities which is simply to change the way you account for existing transactions. Look at the balance sheet chart and imagine increasing the size of the box labelled 'this year's retained profit'. What would you have to do to make the balance sheet balance? You have three choices:

1. Increase one of the assets

2. Decrease one of the liabilities

3. Decrease a previous year's retained profit

We can thus summarise the creative accountant's options as follows:

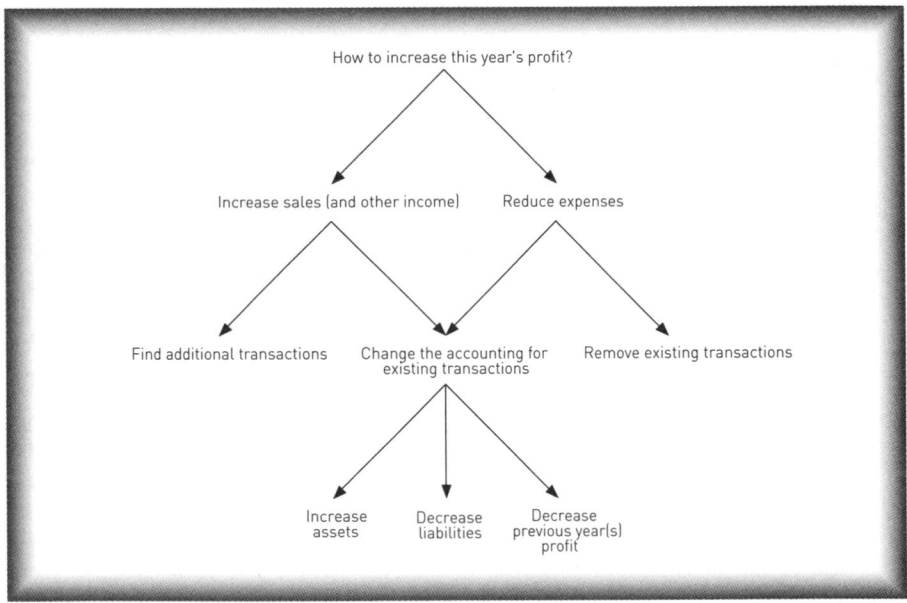

Figure 12.2 The creative accountant's options

How can you change last year's profit? That is surely done and dusted.

Well, you can actually, in special circumstances. In fact, sometimes companies are required by the authorities to restate previous years' accounts. More likely is that, at the end of the *previous* year, a company knows that the following year (i.e. the current year) is going to be difficult, so it finds ways to reduce profits that year. Those profits can then be made to appear in the current year.

So looking at this another way, let's say I buy some goods for cash. I would reduce cash on the assets bar. Instead of reducing this year's retained profit, I would try to find ways to either increase an asset or decrease either liabilities or a previous year's retained profit.

Exactly; and if you want to phrase it in terms of debits and credits, you would say that you have credited cash and should therefore debit this year's retained profit. Instead, you would be looking to debit an asset or one of the other claims.

You will hear people use phrases like 'capitalising an expense' or 'putting it in the balance sheet'. All they mean is that an expense which ought to reduce retained profit (and hence appear in the P&L) actually increases fixed assets. It then appears as a reduction in retained profit in future years when it is depreciated. This is one the most common and easiest tricks of the trade, which I will mention again shortly. Let's now talk about some of the others in more detail.

I've made a list for you of a few tricks which, within the last five years alone, listed companies in the UK and/or the USA have been caught using:

	Increases turnover	Increases profit
1. Delivery made in time but customer not obliged to pay	✓	✓
2. Delivery made in time but before date specified in contract with customer	✓	✓
3. Delivery made in time but customer not obliged to pay for a very long time	✓	✓
4. Delivery made in time but product unserviceable	✓	✓
5. Delivery not made in full before year end but recognised in full anyway	✓	✓
6. Delivery not made before year end but contracts backdated to appear as if it was	✓	✓
7. Early recognition of turnover and profit on long-term contracts	✓	✓
8. Including turnover that should have been included in the previous year's turnover	✓	✓
9. Fabricating sales invoices	✓	✓
10. Treating discounts on expenditure as turnover	✓	✗
11. Treating non-trading income as turnover	✓	✗
12. 'Grossing up' turnover	✓	✗
13. Treating as turnover the sale of product or assets to a company in the same group.	✓	✗
14. Barter deals	✓	✗✓
15. Capitalising expenses	✗	✓
16. Depreciating assets over too long a period	✗	✓
17. Failing to write down fixed assets that are no longer of use to the company	✗	✓
18. Making inadequate provisions against working capital assets	✗	✓
19. 'Writing back' provisions made in previous years	✗	✓
20. Pension holidays	✗	✓
21. Hiding a purchase of goods or services	✗	✓
22. Overstating stock levels	✗	✓
23. Lowering today's expenses in return for something (undisclosed) in the future via side-letter	✗	✓
24. Reducing apparent operating expenses by setting other income (e.g. profit on sale of fixed assets) against them	✗	✓
25. Normalising earnings	✗	✓

Table 12.1 Creative accounting tricks

As you will see, some of these tricks are merely issues of judgment where companies have not chosen the most conservative policy; others are quite clearly deliberate, pre-meditated fraud.

Turnover tricks

You remember when we talked about the phone card you sold to a friend and we discussed when the profit was actually made [page 71]. You concluded rightly, Tom, that the profit was made on the Tuesday when you handed over the card. This is the normal basis for turnover (and therefore cost and profit) recognition. If you haven't delivered the product or service by your financial year end, then you have to put it in next year's accounts. This is pretty simple and it's not hard to judge which year particular sales really belong in. Nonetheless, this has not always stopped directors trying a variety of tricks to make turnover higher in a particular year.

Trick 1 : Delivery made in time but customer not obliged to pay

You deliver large amounts of product to your customers before the year end, having agreed with them that they can return any product that they are unable to sell on to their customers. In this case, the customers would typically be retailers or distributors. They have no real reason not to accommodate you, particularly if you have also told them they don't have to pay for any product until they sell it. Inevitably, lots of the product is returned unpaid-for the following year.

Sometimes, these promises to the customers will be made by a side-letter from a senior director and will not be known to anyone else in the company or to the auditors. As far as everyone else is concerned, there-fore, these are perfectly normal sales which should be booked in the accounts.

Even if the promises are common knowledge, you would still account for the sales normally but would make a provision for some of the

product being returned unpaid-for. This opens the door to 'judgment' and you book the lowest level of provision you can get your auditors to accept.

Trick 2 : Delivery made in time but before date specified in contract with customer

If you have agreed with your customer to deliver in January and your financial year end is 31 December, you might decide to send the product to the customer in December, thereby allowing you to put it in December's sales. Depending on who holds the power in your relationship with your customer, they might accept this without complaint.

Trick 3 : Delivery made in time but customer not obliged to pay for a very long time

If you tell a customer they need not pay for, say, a year, provided they take the product before the year end, they might well decide that that's a great deal even though they don't actually need the product for months (and would, therefore, not normally have ordered it for months).

Trick 4 : Delivery made in time but product unserviceable

Let's suppose you produce bespoke product (e.g. software) for your customers. The year end is approaching so you deliver it to the company even though you know it is not working properly. When the customer complains, you merely talk about 'bugs' or 'snags' being 'normal' and promise to fix it. The sale, however, remains in the current year.

Trick 5 : Delivery not made in full before year end but recognised in full anyway

The classic cheat here is with maintenance contracts on equipment or software. Usually, customers have to pay for these a year in advance. You therefore 'book' all the turnover on the day the year's contract starts. However, at that point, the service has not actually been deliv-

ered. You should only include in the current year that portion of the contract which has been completed by the year end.

Trick 6 : Delivery not made before year end but contracts/invoices backdated to appear as if it was

Pretty self-explanatory, very easy to do for at least a few days after the year end, extremely commonplace.

Trick 7 : Early recognition of turnover and profit on long-term contracts

Some companies undertake work for customers which will take several years to complete. Under the rules, you have to estimate the proportion of the contract that is completed by the year end and what profit you have made at that point. If this is not clear, you have to assume the profit is zero. If you believe you will make a loss on the contract, you have to recognise the *whole* loss in that year.

Obviously, the estimates required (and the need to forecast future events) leave substantial scope for the creative accountant, albeit more in respect of profit than of turnover.

Trick 8 : Including turnover that should have been included in the previous year's turnover

Sometimes, towards the end of the *previous* year, you know you have already achieved your turnover and profit targets. It therefore suits you to delay any new sales until after the year end so that they appear in *this* year's profit. Even if you can't delay an actual sale, you can find ways to justify making a provision against the sale (e.g. asserting that the customer might be unable to pay). When they do pay, during the current year, you can recognise the sale in the current year.

This trick works particularly well when you make an acquisition of another company. If you can get them to hold back sales until after the date the deal is formally completed, then those sales will show up as

'your' sales when you consolidate their accounts in with yours. You thus get yourself a bit of a 'buffer' in the first, often problematic, year of an acquisition.

Trick 9 : Fabricating sales invoices

A lot less trouble and cheaper than fabricating actual product and finding customers for it. Unfortunately, likely to end in a jail sentence for the perpetrators. Amazingly, even this risk has not stopped senior executives of billion dollar, listed companies.

Would the auditors not pick this up, Chris?

More often than not they would, as their procedures include writing to customers who owe you money and asking them to confirm that they do actually owe the sum shown on your debtors ledger. However, remember that in the UK, companies publish their results every six months and in the USA every three months. It is only the year end results that are audited. Thus companies can take liberties with their interim figures that they could not get away with in their year end accounts. Clearly, their goal is to achieve the analysts' expectations of their interim numbers and make up the difference before the year end, by which time all imaginary sales would have been removed from the accounts.

Trick 10 : Treating discounts on expenditure as turnover

If you buy, say, a few million pounds' worth of vehicles over a period of time, your supplier might well agree to give you a retrospective discount when your spending had reached a certain level.

What you should do is account for this discount as a reduction in the cost of the vehicles to which it related. What has been known, however, is for the discount to be treated as turnover.

That seems pretty odd but, presumably, this doesn't really affect profit because you are replacing what would be a lower cost with a higher turnover?

Even if that were true, it still wouldn't make it acceptable, as overstating turnover is still misleading your shareholders. However, it is actually worse than that because, by recognising it as turnover, the company can take the benefit of the discount all in one financial year. If they were to account for it properly, the cost reduction would come in the form of reduced depreciation which would therefore show up in the P&L over a period of years. Obviously, over the full period of the depreciation, the total profit impact is the same, it's just a question of which years' profits it appears in.

Trick 11 : Treating non-trading income as turnover

There are legitimate forms of income other than sales that a company earns which do bring the full benefit in the year in which they occur. These would include income from investments such as interest on cash in the bank or dividends on shares held. If they have nothing to do with the actually trade of the company, however, they should not be treated as turnover but as other income. Companies do, however, sometimes include them in turnover.

So this time there is no effect on the year's profit. What's the point?

Simply because analysts and investors do look at turnover growth as an indication of how well a company is doing and companies naturally try to 'manage' the turnover line. In the madness of the dot com boom, of course, companies had no profits and were being valued using turnover and turnover growth figures, so it was particularly important.

Trick 12 : 'Grossing up' turnover

Imagine your business is to take in product from clients, do something with that product and then deliver it to your clients' customers when they place an order. The client pays you a small fee, perhaps a percentage commission, for doing this. In these circumstances, you would record the fee as your turnover. The reason for this is that you are not

actually buying the product and then selling it on to the end-customer – you are acting as an agent.

Assume then that you change the paperwork a bit with one of these clients so that you are technically buying the product and selling it on to the end-customers. You would then record as turnover the full price the end-customer pays you and as expenses the cost of buying the product from what was your client and is now effectively your supplier.

This doesn't actually change your profit at all but it gives you a higher turnover and matching higher costs. Again, in a world where analysts are looking at turnover growth, this can be a tempting trick if the circumstances are right.

Trick 13 : Treating as turnover the sale of product or assets to a company in the same group

The rules on the accounts for groups of companies are pretty simple in principle. The aim is to present them as if it was all one company. On that basis, you would think that it was pretty clear that you couldn't transfer product or assets from one group company to another and call that turnover.

This has, however, been done on the basis that the transfers were arms' length and it was necessary to report the sales as turnover to give a 'true and fair view'.

Trick 14 : Barter deals

If I agree to sell something to you for £x and you agree to sell me something for £x (even though neither of us has any particular reason for wanting the things we are buying), then we would both artificially raise our turnover without any significant cost or even effort.

If the things we were buying could be defined as assets, we would also both raise our profits for the year as we would have 100 per cent of £x as turnover and only a portion of £x (in the form of depreciation) as our cost.

Expense tricks

The turnover tricks we have just talked about are basically *all* cons, even though some are more obviously breaking the law than others. As I said earlier, there is very little room for doubt over what is and isn't appropriate turnover. There is more genuine scope for judgement in expense tricks, although as we will see, there are many that are just as fraudulent as some of the turnover tricks.

Trick 15 : Capitalising expenses

We talked about this earlier when discussing the generic ways to massage profit. In 2002, Worldcom, a US telecoms company valued at its peak at more than $180bn (that's $180,000,000,000) was famously caught doing this to the tune of more than $4bn of expenses and shortly thereafter went bust.

Here's how it works. Assume you spend $4bn (in cash) renting telephone capacity on networks around the world. You then sell telephone capacity to companies and individuals around the world. Your cash has gone down by $4bn. What else on your balance sheet changes? It should be retained profit for the year as the expense has been incurred and you have nothing to show for it (i.e. no asset), so you should reduce retained profit by $4bn.

If, however, you can persuade yourself that actually, by spending all this money on this network capacity, you have created an asset (which might, in your mind, be the goodwill towards your company of all those happy customers using your huge telephone capacity), you might choose to raise fixed assets by $4bn instead of reducing retained profit.

While the Worldcom case seems a pretty clear cut case of creative accounting, this whole area of what expenditure should and shouldn't be capitalised is a tricky one. Take, for example, software that you employ people to write for use internally (i.e. to enable you to provide your services or manufacture product more efficiently rather than to

sell to customers). The rules say that you have to expense the cost of those people in the current year, even though the software might still be in use by you five years from now.

If, on the other hand, you had commissioned a third party company to write the software for you, you could have capitalised it (i.e. called it an asset) and depreciated it over, say, five years. Thus, again, two identical companies could have very different profit profiles just by taking a different view of how to get their software written.

Trick 16 : Depreciating assets over too long a period

Obviously, if you depreciate an asset over eight years, say, rather than four, you are going to have an annual depreciation charge in the current year that is half what it would otherwise be.

And presumably that is true for the first four years but in years five to eight you are still going to have a depreciation charge when otherwise you wouldn't have any?

Correct. When an asset is fully depreciated and therefore you no longer have that expense in the P&L each year, we say it has gone 'ex-depreciation'.

Trick 17 : Failing to write down fixed assets that are no longer of use to the company

All too often, a company buys an asset and chooses a reasonable depreciation period for it. Subsequently, however, due to a change in the company's business or technology or the condition of the asset or whatever, that asset is no longer of use. At that point, you should write it off – i.e. depreciate it to zero and take the full cost of that depreciation in the current year.

Frequently, companies will look for reasons not to make such write offs and to keep treating the asset as if it were fully productive. Obviously, this avoids denting the current year's profits.

Trick 18 : Making inadequate provisions against working capital assets

There are two main working capital assets : trade debtors (what your customers owe you) and stock. You nearly always have to have provisions against these assets because there's always one customer who can't pay you and you always have some stock which goes bad, gets lost or stolen or becomes obsolete.

These provisions end up as an expense for the year – reduce the asset, reduce retained profit. Obviously, if you understate the provisions, the expense in your P&L for the year will be smaller.

Trick 19 : 'Writing back' provisions made in previous years

If, *last year*, your profits were higher than analysts were expecting, you might decide to make a very large provision against trade debtors or stock, thereby lowering profits to nearer the analysts' expectations. If then, in the current year, that provision turns out to have been *too* large, you simply 'reverse' it – increase the asset, increase retained profit. That profit shows up in this year, so you have neatly transferred some of last year's profit into this year.

Another common way to attempt this massaging is with restructuring costs. You might decide to undergo a major restructuring of all or part of your business. This often happens after a company makes an acquisition or when it is in trouble and a new management team has arrived to try to sort it out.

What you do is say, towards the end of the year: 'We are going to have to re-organise this business next year and incur all these costs in doing so. We must allow for them in this year's accounts. We will therefore

make a provision and accept a large exceptional cost in our retained profit. Next year, surprise, surprise, the actual costs of the reorganisation will not be as high as we thought so we will "release" some of the provision. Of course, the re-organisation takes a long time so we will probably have to hold off releasing some of the provisions into the year after next and release it then'. This enables you to transfer some profit from this year into next year and the year after.

The rules now say that you have to have a detailed formal plan in place and a reasonable expectation among those people who are affected that the re-organisation will happen. As you can imagine, this merely reduces the level of abuse rather than stopping it all together.

In passing, you might make a mental note that this is the second trick where I have mentioned acquisitions. In general, making an acquisition adds to the complexity of a company's accounting and gives the company more scope for creative accounting. Some acquisitive companies have created huge value for their shareholders. Many others have soared for a while before crashing back down again.

Trick 20 : Pension holidays

Where a company's pension fund has sufficient assets in it to meet its liabilities to the company's pensioners, the company can reduce its payments into the fund, thereby enhancing profits for a number of years. Nowadays, the notes to the accounts will tell you this has been done so you just need to be aware of it.

Trick 21 : Hiding a purchase of goods or services

Suppose you have to hire some temporary labour from an agency to help complete some work for a customer. In normal circumstances, the labour supplier will send you an invoice which will appear on your creditors' ledger. The auditors will, as they do with debtors, write to creditors to check that the amounts you say you owe are the amounts the creditors think they are owed.

Suppose, however, that you take that labour from an agency you have never used before and get them to agree (by paying a high price for the labour) not to press for payment for six months. Then, by simply hiding the paperwork, the auditors are never going to know of your relationship with that supplier and the fact that that expense exists. It will never get into this year's accounts. Of course, you will have to put it in next year's accounts but you'll have sorted all your problems out by next year, won't you?

Trick 22 : Overstating stock levels

If you are desperate, you can go further with stock than simply playing around with provisions. You find ways to make the gross value of your stock (i.e. before any provisions) seem higher than it is.

How does that help profits?

As follows. Remember when SBL sold some stock, we recognised the turnover and then said we had to remove the stock from our balance sheet as we no longer owned that stock. The cost of that stock appeared as a reduction in retained profit. If we could get away with NOT recognising all that cost in retained profit, we would have higher profit.

Yes, but how would you do that? If you have sold the stock, you have sold the stock, haven't you?

True, but remember our conversation about FIFO and Average as ways of accounting for stock sold? There are different, but perfectly acceptable ways to account for stock. If you change from one to the other during a year, there will almost certainly be some impact on your accounts.

The other thing you should remember is that companies' records are not always perfect. In fact, they are often a long way from perfect. So the way auditors check whether the right value of stock has been

expensed is by physically checking the stock at the year end. They can then calculate, based on what was there at the beginning of the year and how much the company has bought during the year, how much has actually been sold (or lost, stolen or whatever).

I'm not sure I get this, Chris.

OK. Take a company that buys and sells oil. If you know they have 20m gallons at the start of the year, and that they bought 240m gallons during the year and that they have 40m gallons left at the end of the year, then you know they must have sold (or lost or had stolen or spoiled)

$$20m + 240m - 40m = 220m \text{ gallons}$$

If you are using the averaging method, you can then place a monetary value on the stock and hence on the cost of sales. The trick for the accounts manipulator therefore is to make the stock appear as large as possible at the year end. In terms of the balance sheet chart, what we have done here is make the balance sheet balance by raising the left hand bar rather than lowering the right hand bar.

So how do you actually make the stock look larger at the year end than it is?

A number of ways have been tried, including :

- Asserting that some stock, which you have ordered and have been invoiced for, has not actually yet been received by you and therefore adding it to your stock value;

- Moving stock from warehouse to warehouse while the auditors are doing their stock check so they count the same stock twice;

- Buying stock from a new supplier and hiding all the paperwork until the audit is completed (i.e. a version of trick 21).

Trick 23 : Lowering today's expenses in return for something (undisclosed) in the future via side-letter

You make an agreement with your suppliers that, in return for low prices this year, you will pay much higher prices next year or the year after or whenever. This agreement, however, you make in a side-letter, which is legally binding on you but which the auditors and perhaps members of your staff never see. You can thus record good profits this year due to the low cost of product, albeit that you will get hit hard in future years.

Trick 24 : Reducing apparent operating expenses by setting other income (e.g. profit on sale of fixed assets) against them

Sell off an asset which is fully depreciated in your books and you will have a profit equal to the proceeds of the sale. Provided it is not so large that you have to disclose it as an exceptional item, you just 'bury' that profit in one of the expense lines so it looks like your expenses are lower than they actually are.

But you are still recording the correct profit aren't you?

Yes, but the *source* of profit is obviously important to understanding how sustainable a company's performance is. After all, you can't keep selling assets off every year to make up for not being able to make enough profit in your real business.

Trick 25 : Normalising earnings

Under the new rules, companies have to show the calculation of earnings per share including *all* costs in their calculation of earnings. The problem with this is that if a company has some genuine exceptional or extraordinary costs (or income), the trend in earnings per share is distorted.

Companies are, therefore, allowed to present a second calculation of earnings per share, excluding any items they consider exceptional or extraordinary, provided they explain the differences between the two calculations.

The trouble for the investor is that companies tend to remove costs they deem out of the ordinary but leave in any such income, thereby inflating earnings per share. You can see the costs they have excluded but you simply don't know if there are any out of the ordinary income amounts which should have been excluded as well.

That's probably enough of tricks. The last thing I should point out is that companies can do the exact opposite of each of these tricks to lower profit in the current year so as to make it higher in future years. If the current year has been particularly good or lucky, this may suit them. As an investor, you are lulled into thinking the company is continuing to do well when in fact the situation is deteriorating.

Spotting creative accounting

This is all a bit frightening, Chris. How do you tell when companies are playing these tricks?

The answer is that it depends. We can put these tricks into three categories:

- **Those you have no clue about until it is too late**
  This would include things like hiding purchase invoices or writing undisclosed side-letters.

- **Those which show up in the accounts**
  For example, if a company sells product on 'sale or return', this will be disclosed in the notes. This doesn't mean that they are cheating but the scope for them to do so is there.

  A lot of the tricks we have been talking about can be used by companies from the day they start trading. More often than not, however,

companies start using them when they need to. This tends to be just before they are floated on a stock exchange and need their numbers to look good or pretty much any time after they have floated and they are looking like missing the analysts' forecasts.

Frequently, therefore, tricks are flagged by the company having to declare changes in accounting policies. Whenever you see ANY change in accounting policy, then the words 'rat' and 'smell' should spring rapidly to mind. If you see several policy changes in one year, or any one policy changes more than once within a few years, you should probably be looking elsewhere for an investment.

Watch also for changes in auditors, the company's year end, the finance director, etc. Any such change should make you ask questions.

- **Those you identify through your own analysis**
  If you carry out the analyses we have talked about over the last couple of days, you will see odd things happening when some of these tricks are being played. In particular, focus on trade debtors and stock. If debtors are rising much more quickly than sales or debtor days are just very high, you should start asking questions. It may just be that that company has a problem collecting debts, although that is pretty serious in itself from a cash point of view, but it may be that they are booking 'imaginary' sales which they cannot actually collect cash for. Likewise if stock turn is high or has risen sharply recently, you should start worrying.

Why bother?

But there are so many of these tricks. Being realistic, we're not going to be able to check for all of them. Is it worth even bothering with the accounts?

Without question, yes. There are lots of companies out there you can invest in. Many of them will be indulging in a bit of gentle massaging

of their results but very few are taking some of the extreme measures we have talked about. Remember, after all, that most of these tricks are now outlawed by the accounting standards and I expect the punishments for directors who break the rules are going to become more severe in light of the recent scandals.

What you are trying to do with the accounts is to reduce the chances of investing your hard-earned cash in one of the relatively few extreme cases. You do know enough now to do this.

Remember the following:

- Never rely on the main financial statements without referring to the notes.

- Never draw conclusions from just one parameter.

- Never rely on the company's own calculations of ratios. Their definitions may be different.

- Keep asking yourself the question 'why?' This will make you keep digging a little deeper.

- Always look for trends and sudden changes.

- Try to get comparative information for companies in the same industry.

- Look for reasons not to make an investment – there are plenty of other companies

Fine, but is there nothing we can look for in the accounts to actually support making an investment in a company?

If you twisted my arm, I would give you three things to focus on – but remember you can't rely on these things alone.

Look for simplicity

When reading the annual reports of a company, ask yourself if you *really* understand what it does? The days when companies just made things and sold them are over. We now have all sorts of new 'business models', as the bankers call them.

The greatest investor of our time, Warren Buffett, has made himself a multi-billionaire investing in simple businesses he understands and steering clear of new technologies and new 'models'.

Return on capital employed (ROCE)

As we saw earlier, ROCE is the ultimate measure of the enterprise's financial performance. A company which is consistently delivering a high return on capital employed is definitely worthy of consideration. Some of the most successful companies have been those whose internal financial strategy is focused on ROCE.

This is a less useful measure in 'people' businesses where there is often a low capital requirement but there are still plenty of traditional businesses where the measure makes sense and provides a good indication of the quality of the company and its management.

Remember that this takes account of both profit and capital employed, so if a company is artificially inflating profit by tricks which lead to high debtors, stock or fixed assets, then ROCE will reflect the effect of these tricks.

Because the capital employed will be higher and therefore ROCE will be lower?

Exactly. If I can be cynical again for a second, remember that companies' working capital goes up and down during the course of a year – particularly in companies whose business is very seasonal. Companies therefore pick the date for their year end which flatters their results the most. Furthermore, large companies in particular often stop paying creditors for the last few weeks of their financial year so their cash position looks better at the balance sheet date.

Cash flow

Regardless of the business, my final recommendation is to get to understand the cash flow statement. I like this statement for two reasons.

- First, and most importantly, you can't massage cash the way you can profits. Cash is either there or it isn't (although you do need to be a bit cautious if a lot of cash is being generated in dubious foreign currencies).

- Second, because of the categories required in a modern cash flow statement, it makes it a lot easier to separate the cash characteristics of the enterprise from the funding structure.

Look for companies where the enterprise is generating cash consistently (and preferably where cash flow is rising steadily). There are no guarantees but this suggests good operating and financial management. Excess cash flows through into share values either through high dividend payouts or re-investment in the enterprise which should produce additional profit and cash flow.

> ## SUMMARY
>
> - Company accounts are designed to show the company in the best light possible and should therefore be read in a cynical frame of mind.
> - Keep asking yourself: "why?"
> - The rules have been and continue to be tightened up but cases of abuse go on.
> - In the particularly bad cases, shareholders can lose all of their investment, so don't put all your money into one company.
> - The golden rule of investment is:
>
>   *If in doubt, don't invest.*

Glossary

Synonyms are shown in **_bold italics_** in brackets

Accounting period   The time between two consecutive *balance sheet dates* (and therefore the period to which the *profit and loss account* and *cash flow* statement relate).

Accounting policies   The specific methods chosen by companies to account for certain items (e.g. stock, depreciation) subject to the guidelines of the *accounting standards*.

Accounting standards   The accounting rules and guidelines issued by the recognised authority (currently the *Accounting Standards Board*).

Accounting Standards Board (ASB)   The body currently responsible for *accounting standards*. Find out more at www.ASB.org.uk.

Accounting Standards Committee (ASC)   The body formerly responsible for *accounting standards* (prior to the formation of the *Accounting Standards Board*).

Accounts payable (_Trade creditors_)   The amount a company owes to its suppliers at any given moment.

Accounts receivable (_Trade debtors_)   The amount a company is owed by its customers at any given moment.

Accrual   Adjustment made at the end of an *accounting period* to *recognise expenses* that have been incurred during the period but for which no *invoice* has yet been issued.

Accruals concept   Under the accruals concept, *revenues* are *recognised* when goods or services are delivered, not when payment for those goods or services is received. Similarly, all *expenses* incurred to generate the revenues of a given *accounting period* are recognised, irrespective of whether payment has been made or not.

Accumulated depreciation/amortisation   The total *depreciation* or *amortisation* of an asset since the asset was purchased.

Allotted share capital (*Issued share capital*)   The amount of the *authorised share capital* that has actually been allotted to investors.

Amortisation   The amount by which the *book value* of an *intangible asset* (including goodwill) is deemed to have fallen during a particular *accounting period*.

Annual report and accounts (*Annual report*)   The report issued annually to *shareholders* containing the *directors' report*, the *auditors' report* and the financial statements for the year.

'A' Share   Usually refers to a share which has a right to a proportion of a company's *assets* but no voting rights.

Asset   Anything of value which a company owns or is owed.

Associated undertaking (*Associate*)   Broadly speaking, a company is an associate of an investor company if it is not a *subsidiary* but the investor company exerts a significant influence over the company. 'Significant influence' is normally assumed to occur when the investor holds in excess of 20 per cent of the company.

Audit   Annual inspection of a company's *books* and financial statements carried out by *auditors*.

Auditors   Accountants appointed to carry out a company's *audit.*

Auditors' report   Report on a company's financial statements prepared for the *shareholders* by the *auditors*.

Audit trail   Module of all accounting systems which records in chronologic order the details of every transaction posted to the system

Authorised share capital   The total number of shares the directors of a company have been authorised by the *shareholders* to issue.

Average method   Method of accounting for *stock* whereby, if a company has identical items of stock which cost different amounts to buy or produce, the average value is used.

Bad debt   Money owed by a customer which will never be paid.

Balance sheet   Statement of a company's *assets* and the *claims* over those assets at any given moment (i.e. at the *balance sheet date*).

Balance sheet date   Date at which a *balance sheet* is drawn up.

Balance sheet equation   Statement of the *fundamental principle of accounting*, whereby the *assets* of a company must equal the *claims* over those assets (i.e. the *liabilities* and *shareholders' equity*).

Benchmarking   Method of assessing a company's performance by comparing it against competitors or other benchmarks.

Bond (*Long-term loan, Loanstock*)   A *loan* which is not due to be repaid for at least twelve months. More specifically, the bond is the certificate showing the amount and terms of the loan.

Books   The records of all the *transactions* of a company and the effect of those transactions on the company's financial position.

Book value   The value that an *asset* has in a company's books. The book value of an asset is usually different from its *market value*.

Capital and reserves (*Equity, Shareholders' equity/funds*)   The share of a company's *assets* that are 'due' to the *shareholders*. Consists of *share capital*, *share premium*, *retained profit*, and any other *reserves*.

Capital allowance   When calculating *taxable income*, the Inland Revenue takes no account of *depreciation* on *tangible fixed assets*. Instead, capital allowances are made which reduce taxable income (effectively, capital allowances are the Inland Revenue's method of depreciation).

Capital employed (*Net operating assets*)   The total amount of money tied up in a business in the form of *fixed assets* and *working capital*. It is also equal to the sum of the *equity*, the *debt* and any *corporation tax* payable.

Capital expenditure   Money spent on *fixed assets* as opposed to day to day running expenses.

Capital structure (*Financial structure, Funding structure*)   The relative proportions of the funding for a company that are provided by *debt* and *equity*.

Capital productivity   *Sales* divided by *capital employed*.

Cash flow   The change in a company's cash balance over a particular period.

Cash in flow statement   A statement showing the reasons behind a company's *cash flow* during a particular *accounting period*.

Cash in advance (*Deferred revenue/income*)   Cash received as payment for goods or services before those goods or services have been provided remains a *liability* to the customer until the goods or services are provided.

Charge (*Lien*)   First claim over an *asset* (normally taken as *security* for a *loan*).

Class of share   Different types of *shares* are described as being different classes.

Commercial paper   A form of *short-term loan* issued by companies requiring funds.

Consolidated accounts   Accounts prepared for a *parent company* and its *subsidiaries* as if the parent company and the subsidiaries were all just one company.

Contingent liability   A *liability* which may or may not arise depending on the outcome of some future event.

Convertible loanstock/bond   A *loan* which the lender can convert into *shares* in the company rather than accepting repayment of the loan.

Convertible preference share   A *preference share* which can be converted by the holder into *ordinary shares* in the company.

Corporation tax   The tax paid by a company on its profits.

Cost of goods sold (*Cost of sales*)   All materials costs and *expenses* which can be directly ascribed to the production of the goods sold.

Coupon   (1) The *interest* payable on a *bond*.
             (2) The *dividend* payable on a *preference share*.

Covenant   Restriction imposed by a lender, breach of which normally enables the lender to demand immediate repayment of the *debt*.

Credit   (1) Time given to a customer to pay for goods or services supplied.
             (2) In *double entry book-keeping*, there are always at least two entries; one of these is always a credit, the other is always a *debit*.

Creditor   Someone who is owed money, goods or services.

Cumulative preference shares *Preference shares* with the additional condition that, if any *preference dividends* for past years have not been paid, these must be paid in full before a *dividend* can be paid to the *ordinary shareholders*.

Current asset An *asset* that is expected to be turned into cash within one year of the *balance sheet date*.

Current cost convention Accounting convention whereby *assets* are recorded in a company's *books* based on their *market value* or replacement cost at the *balance sheet date*.

Current liability A *liability* that is expected to be paid within one year of the *balance sheet date*.

Current ratio *Current assets* divided by *current liabilities*.

Debenture A *long-term loan* issued by a company, usually with *security* over some or all of the company's *assets*.

Debit In *double-entry book-keeping*, there are always at least two entries; one of these is always a *credit*, the other is always a *debit*.

Debt (1) Money, goods or services owed.
(2) Any funding which has a known rate of *interest* and *term*. Typically, a form of *loan* or *overdraft*.

Debtor Someone who owes money, goods or services.

Debt to equity ratio (*Gearing*) *Debt* divided by *equity*.

Debt to total funding ratio *Debt* divided by the sum of debt and *equity*.

Deferred revenue/income (*Cash in advance*) Cash received as payment for goods or services before those goods or services have been provided. Since the goods or services have not been provided, the revenue can not yet be *recognised*, i.e. it is deferred.

Deferred shares   Typically, *shares* that have voting rights but no rights to a *dividend* until certain conditions are met (e.g. profits reach a specified level).

Deferred taxation   *Corporation tax* on a particular year's profits which the company does not have to pay in the coming year but which it expects to have to pay at some date in the future.

Depreciation   The amount by which the *book value* of a *tangible fixed asset* is deemed to have fallen during a particular *accounting period*. Depreciation therefore appears as an *expense* of that period.

Directors' report   Report on a company's affairs by the directors (included as part of the *annual report*).

Distribution   Payment of a *dividend* to *shareholders* (thereby 'distributing' some of the profits of the company).

Dividend   Payment made to *shareholders* out of the *retained profit* of the company.

Dividend cover   *Profit for the year* divided by the *dividend* payable.

Dividend yield   A company's *dividend* per *share* for a year divided by the *share price*. Alternatively, the total dividends for the year divided by the *market capitalisation* of the company.

Double-entry book-keeping   Procedure for recording *transactions* whereby at least two entries are made on the *balance sheet*, thereby enabling the balance sheet to remain 'in balance'.

Doubtful debt   Money due to a company which the company is not reasonably confident of receiving.

Earnings before interest and tax (EBIT) (*Profit before interest and tax, Trading profit, Operating profit*)   The profit generated by the *enterprise* of a company, i.e. profit before taking account of *interest* (either payable or receivable) and *corporation tax*.

Earnings (*Profit for the year*)   Profit attributable to *ordinary share-holders* (after taking account of *corporation tax, minority interests, extraordinary items, preference dividends* but before taking account of any *ordinary dividends* payable).

Earnings dilution   Reduction in *earnings per share* as a result of the company issuing new *shares*.

Earnings per share   *Earnings* divided by the average number of *ordinary shares* in issue during the *accounting period*.

Equity (*Capital and reserves, Shareholders' equity/funds*)   The share of a company's *assets* that are 'due' to the *shareholders*. Consists of *share capital, share premium, retained profit*, and any other *reserves*. For the purposes of financial analysis, *dividends* can be included in equity. 'Equity' is also used more loosely to mean any funding raised by a company in return for *shares*.

Equity method   Method of accounting for *associates* whereby the *investment* is shown on the investor's *balance sheet* as the investor's share of the *net assets* of the associate.

Enterprise   The actual business of a company, i.e. the components of the company which are unaffected by the *funding structure* (the way in which the funding for the company was raised).

Exceptional item   Any item that is part of the ordinary activities of a company but which, because of its size or nature, needs to be disclosed if the financial statements are to give a true and fair view.

Exchange gain/loss   Gain or loss made as a result solely of the movement in the exchange rate between two currencies.

Exercising an option   The activation of an *option* to buy or sell the *shares* to which the option relates.

Exercise price   The price paid or received when buying or selling the relevant *share* as a result of *exercising an option*.

Expense   Any cost incurred which reduces the profits of a particular *accounting period* (as opposed to *capital expenditure* or *prepayments*, for example).

Extraordinary item   Any expense or income which falls outside the ordinary activities of a company and is not expected to recur.

Final dividend   *Dividend* declared at the end of a company's *fiscal year*. Has to be approved by the *shareholders*.

Finance lease   A *lease* where the *lessee* (i.e. the user of the *asset*) has the vast majority of the risks and rewards of ownership of the asset, i.e. the lessee effectively owns the asset. For accounting purposes, finance leases are treated as if the lessee had actually bought the asset with a *loan* from the *lessor*.

Financial Reporting Standards (FRS)   The *accounting standards* issued by the *Accounting Standards Board*.

Financial structure (*Capital structure, Funding structure*)   The relative proportions of the funding for a company that are provided by *debt* and *equity*.

First in first out   Method of accounting for *stock* whereby, if a company has identical items of stock which cost different amounts to buy or produce, the oldest stock is assumed to be used first.

Fiscal year   The year preceding the *balance sheet date* (used for reporting a company's results to its *shareholders*).

Fixed asset   An *asset* used by a company on a long-term continuing basis (as opposed to assets which are used up in a short period of time or are bought to be sold on to customers).

Fixed asset productivity   *Sales* divided by the *net book value* of *fixed assets*.

Fixed charge   A *charge* over a specific *asset* of a company.

Fixed cost   An *expense* which does not change with small changes in the volume of goods produced (examples might include rent, rates, insurance etc.).

Floating charge   A *charge* over all the *assets* of a company rather than any specific asset.

Forward P/E (*Prospective P/E*)   The *price earnings ratio* calculated using a forecast of the coming year's *earnings*.

Fully diluted earnings per share   *Earnings per share* calculated after taking into account unissued *shares* which the company may be forced to issue at some time in the future (as a result of outstanding *options*, *convertible loanstock*, etc.).

Fundamental principle of accounting   The *assets* of a company must always exactly equal the *claims* over those assets.

Funding structure (*Capital structure, Financial structure*)   The relative proportions of the funding for a company that are provided by *debt* and *equity*.

Gearing (*Debt to equity ratio*)   General term used to describe the use of *debt* as well as *equity* to fund a company. The term is used more specifically to describe the ratio of debt to equity.

Going concern concept   One of the basic accounting concepts: when preparing a *balance sheet*, it is assumed that the company will continue in business for the foreseeable future.

Goodwill   In the case of a *subsidiary*, the difference between what an investing company paid for *shares* in the *subsidiary* and the fair value of

the *assets* of the *subsidiary*. In the case of an *associate*, the difference between what an investing company paid for *shares* in the *associate* and the *net book value* of those *shares*.

Gross assets   The total *assets* of a company before deducting any *liabilities*.

Gross margin   *Gross profit* as a percentage of *turnover*.

Gross profit   *Turnover* less *cost of goods sold*.

Hedging currency exposure   Currency transactions undertaken to cancel out the effect of any future movement in the rate of exchange between two currencies to which a company is exposed.

Historical cost convention   Accounting convention whereby *assets* are recorded in a company's *books* based on the price paid for them (as opposed to the *market value* or replacement cost of those assets at the *balance sheet date*).

Historic P/E   The *price earnings ratio* calculated using the most recently reported *earnings* figure.

Input   Raw material, equipment, service, etc. bought in by a company to enable it to produce its *outputs*.

Insolvent   A company is insolvent when it is unable to meet its *liabilities*.

Instrument (*Security*)   General term for any type of *debt* or *equity*.

Intangible asset   A *fixed asset* which cannot be touched (e.g. patents, brand names).

Interest   The amount paid to lenders in return for the use of their money for a period of time.

Interest cover   *Operating profit* divided by *interest* payable.

Interim dividend *Dividend* declared in the course of a company's *fiscal* year.

Inventory (*Stock*) Raw materials, *work in progress* and finished goods.

Investment An *asset* that is not used directly in a company's operations.

Invoice Formal document issued by a supplier company to its customer (recording the details of the *transaction*).

Issued share capital (*Allotted share capital*) The amount of the *authorised share capital* that has actually been issued to investors.

Journal entry End-of-period adjustment to a company's accounts (e.g. to *post accruals* or *depreciation*).

Last in first out Method of accounting for *stock* whereby, if a company has identical items of stock which cost different amounts to buy or produce, the newest stock is assumed to be used first.

Lease An agreement whereby the owner of an asset (the *lessor*) allows someone else (the *lessee*) to use that asset.

Lessee The user of an *asset* which is owned by someone else but is being used by the lessee under the terms of a *lease*.

Lessor The owner of an asset which is being used by someone else under the terms of a *lease*.

Liability Money, goods or services owed by a company.

Lien (*Charge*) First claim over an *asset* (normally taken as *security* for a *loan*).

Limited company A company whose *shareholders* do not have any *liability* to the company's *creditors* above the amount they have paid

into the company as *share capital*. Hence the shareholders have 'limited liability'.

Liquid assets   *Assets* which are either cash or can be turned into cash quickly and easily.

Liquidate   To sell all a company's *assets*, pay off the *liabilities* and pay any remaining cash to the *shareholders*.

Liquidity   The ability of a company to pay its short-term *liabilities*.

Listed company (*Quoted company*)   A company whose *shares* can be bought or sold readily through a recognised *stock exchange*.

Loan   Funding of a fixed amount (unlike an *overdraft*, which varies on a day to day basis), with a known rate of *interest*, an agreed repayment schedule and, usually, a *charge* over some or all of the company's *assets*.

Long-term loan (*Bond, Loanstock*)   A *loan* which is not due to be repaid for at least twelve months.

Long-term liability   Any *liability* which does not have to be settled within the next twelve months.

Marketable   An *asset* is marketable if it can be sold quickly and without affecting the market price of similar assets.

Market capitalisation   The total *market value* of all the *ordinary shares* of a *listed company*.

Market to book ratio   *Market value* of *shares* divided by *book value* of those shares.

Market value   The value of an *asset* to an unconnected third party.

Matching   The process under the *accruals concept* whereby all *expenses* incurred to generate the *sales* of an *accounting period* are *recognised* in the accounts of that period.

Member (*Shareholder*)   Holder of *shares* in a company.

Minority interest   When a *parent company* owns less than 100 per cent of a *subsidiary*, the *consolidated accounts* will identify separately 'minority interests' to show the portion of the *net assets* and the year's profits which are attributable to the owners of the minority shareholding rather than to the *shareholders* of the parent company.

Mortgage   A *charge* over a specific *asset*.

Net assets (*Net worth*)   The total *assets* of a company less its *liabilities*.

Net book value   The value of an *asset* as recorded in the company's *books* after allowing for *accumulated depreciation* or *accumulated amortisation*.

Net operating assets (*Capital employed*)   The total amount of money tied up in a business in the form of *fixed assets* and *working capital*. It is also equal to the sum of the *equity*, the *debt* and any *corporation tax* payable.

Net realisable value   The price which could be obtained if an *asset* were sold (after allowing for all costs associated with the sale). The term is usually applied to valuation of *stock*.

Net worth (*Net assets*)   The total *assets* of a company less its *liabilities*.

Nominal account   Each of the different items that make up a *balance sheet* is a nominal account. In practice, companies often have many hundreds of nominal accounts which are then summarised to produce the balance sheet you see in a company's *annual report*.

Nominal ledger   A book or computer program which records details of each of the *nominal accounts*.

Nominal value (*Par value*)   The face value of a company's *shares*. The company cannot issue shares for less than this value.

Note of historical cost profits and losses   A summary statement showing the additional profit or loss that would have been recorded in the *P&L* if an unrealised gain or loss had not, in a previous year, been recognised and shown in the *statement of recognised gains and losses*.

Notional interest   *Interest* income that would have been earned by a company during a particular *accounting period* if *option* holders had *exercised* their options at the start of that period.

Off-balance sheet finance   Funding raised by a company which does not have to be *recognised* on its *balance sheet*.

Operating cash flow   The change in a company's cash during an *accounting period* due solely to its *enterprise* (i.e. disregarding interest/ tax/dividend payments, equity/debt issues, etc).

Operating expense   *Expense* incurred by the *enterprise* (i.e. excluding all *funding structure* items such as *interest*, tax, etc.).

Operating lease   A *lease* where the *lessee* does not take on substantially all the risks and rewards of ownership of the *asset*.

Operating profit (*Earnings before interest and tax, Profit before interest and tax, Trading profit*)   The profit generated by the *enterprise* of a company; i.e. profit before taking account of *interest* (either payable or receivable) and *corporation tax*.

Option   The right to buy or sell *shares* in a company at a certain price (the *exercise price*) during a certain period.

Ordinary dividend   *Dividend* paid to holders of *ordinary shares*.

Ordinary share   The most common *class* of *share*. Entitles the holder to a proportionate share of *dividends* and *net assets*, and to vote at meetings of the *shareholders*.

Output   The product or service produced by a company.

Overdraft Funding provided by a bank. Unlike a loan, the amount varies on a day to day basis, and is usually repayable on demand. An overdraft carries a known rate of *interest*, and usually the company will have to give the bank a *charge* over some or all of its *assets*.

Overdraft facility Agreed limit of an *overdraft*.

Overheads *Operating expenses* which cannot be directly ascribed to the production of goods or services.

Parent company A company which has one or more *subsidiaries*.

Participating preference share A *preference share* whose *dividend* is increased if the company meets certain performance criteria.

Par value (*Nominal value*) The face value of a company's *shares*. The company cannot issue shares for less than this value.

Payout ratio *Dividends* divided by *profit for the year*.

Petty cash Small amounts of cash held on a company's premises to cover incidental expenses.

Post balance sheet event An event which takes place after the *balance sheet date* but which needs to be disclosed in order that the *annual report* should give a true and fair view of the company's financial position.

Posting Making an entry onto a company's *balance sheet*.

Preference dividend *Dividend* payable on a *preference share*.

Preference share *Share* which has a right to a *dividend* which must be paid in full before the *ordinary shareholders* can be paid a dividend.

Prepayment A payment made in advance of the receipt of goods or services (e.g. a deposit).

Price earnings ratio (PER, P/E)   *Share price* divided by *earnings per share*. Equal to *market capitalisation* divided by *earnings*.

Prior year adjustment   An adjustment to a prior year's *balance sheet*.

Productivity   A measure of output divided by a measure of input (e.g. sales per employee, sales per pound of capital employed).

Profit & loss account   A statement showing how the *retained profit* of a company (as shown on the *balance sheet*) changed during a particular *accounting period*.

Profit after tax   Profit after taking account of all *expenses* including *interest* and *corporation tax* (but before taking account of any *dividends* payable).

Profit before interest and tax (PBIT) (*Earnings before interest and tax, Operating profit, Trading profit*)   The profit generated by the *enterprise* of a company, i.e. profit before taking account of *interest* (either payable or receivable) and *corporation tax*.

Profit before tax (PBT)   Profit after all *expenses* including interest but before *corporation tax*.

Profit for the year (*Earnings*)   Profit attributable to *ordinary shareholders* (after taking account of *corporation tax, minority interests, extraordinary items, preference dividends* but before taking account of any *ordinary dividends* payable).

Profitability   The amount of profit made by a company for each pound of capital invested. Usually measured as *return on capital employed* and/or *return on equity*.

Prospective P/E (*Forward P/E*)   The *price earnings ratio* calculated using a forecast of the coming year's *earnings*.

Provision   An *expense recognised* in the accounts for a particular

accounting period to allow for expected losses (e.g. a *doubtful debt*).

Public limited company (plc)   A *limited company* which is subject to more stringent legal requirements than a private limited company. All *listed companies* are plc's but a plc need not be listed.

Purchase ledger   A book or computer program in which details of suppliers and amounts owed to them are recorded.

Qualified auditors' report   An *auditors' report* which has a qualification to the usual 'true and fair view' statement.

Quick ratio   *Current assets* less *stock* divided by *current liabilities*.

Realisation   Conversion of an *asset* into cash, or a promise of cash which is reasonably certain of being fulfilled.

Recognition   The inclusion of the impact of a *transaction* on a company's *balance sheet*.

Redeemable preference share   *Preference share* which has a fixed *term*, at the end of which the holder's money is returned and the preference share cancelled.

Reserve   A *nominal account*, other than *share capital*, which represents a claim of the *shareholders* of a company over some of the *assets* of the company. Examples include *retained profit* and *revaluation* reserve.

Return on capital employed   *Operating profit* divided by *capital employed*. The key measure of the financial performance of the *enterprise*.

Return on equity   *Profit before tax* divided by *shareholders' equity*. Often calculated using *profit after tax* or *profit for the year*.

Return on sales   *Operating profit* divided by *sales*.

Retained profit/earnings   The total cumulative profits of a company that have been retained (i.e. not distributed to shareholders as dividends).

Revaluation reserve A *reserve* created when the *net assets* of a company are increased due to the revaluation of certain of the company's *assets*.

Revenue The amount due to (or paid to) a company in return for the goods or services supplied by that company. Note that revenue is usually recorded in a company's accounts net of VAT (i.e. after subtracting the VAT element).

Rights issue An issue of new *shares* whereby the *shareholders* have the right to acquire the new shares in proportion to their existing holdings before the shares can be offered to anyone else.

Sales (*Turnover*) The total *revenues* of a company in an *accounting period*.

Sales ledger A book or computer program in which details of customers and amounts owed by them are recorded.

Scrip issue A free issue of additional *shares* to *shareholders* in proportion to their existing holdings. It has no effect on the *market capitalisation* of a company but reduces the price of each share.

Security (1) Rights over certain *assets* of a company given when a *loan* or *overdraft* are granted to the company. If the terms of the loan or overdraft are breached then the rights can normally be exercised to enable the lenders to get their money back.
(2) (*Instrument*) A general term for any type of *equity* or *debt*.

Share One of the equal parts into which any particular *class* of a company's *share capital* is divided. Each share entitles its owner to a proportion of the assets due to that class of share capital.

Share capital The *nominal value* of the *shares* issued by a company. 'Share capital' is also used more generally to describe any funding raised by a company in return for *shares*.

Shareholder (*Member*)   Holder of *shares* in a company.

Shareholders' equity/funds (*Equity, Capital and reserves*)   The share of a company's *assets* that are 'due' to the *shareholders*. Consists of *share capital*, *share premium*, *retained profit*, and any other *reserves*. For the purposes of financial analysis, *dividends* can be included in shareholders' equity.

Share premium   The amount paid for a company's *shares* over and above the *nominal value* of those shares.

Share price   The *market value* of each *share* in a company.

Short-term loan   A *loan* which is due to be repaid within twelve months of the *balance sheet date*.

Statement of recognised gains and losses   A primary financial statement (like the *P&L*, *balance sheet* and *cash flow statement*) that records any gains or losses *recognised* during the financial year but which, because they are not yet *realised*, do not appear in the *P&L*.

Statement of standard accounting practice (SSAP)   The *accounting standards* set by the *Accounting Standards Committee* (*ASC*). The ASC has now been replaced by the *Accounting Standards Board* (*ASB*), whose new standards are known as *Financial Reporting Standards*. The SSAP's remain in force, however, until withdrawn by the ASB.

Stock   (1) Raw materials, *work in progress* and goods ready for sale. (2) In USA, the equivalent of *shares*.

Stock exchange   A market on which a company's *shares* can be *listed* (and therefore be readily bought and sold).

Subordinated loanstock   A *long-term loan* that ranks behind other *creditors*. Thus, if a company is *wound up*, all other *creditors* are paid in full before the subordinated loanstock holders receive anything.

Subsidiary undertaking (*Subsidiary*) Broadly speaking, a company is a subsidiary of another company (the *parent company*) if the parent company owns more than 50 per cent of the voting rights or exerts a dominant influence over the subsidiary.

Tangible fixed asset A *fixed asset* that can be touched, such as property, plant, equipment.

Taxable income The income on which the Inland Revenue calculates the *corporation tax* payable by a company.

Term Duration of a *loan, redeemable preference share* or other *instrument*.

Trade creditors (*Accounts payable*) The amount a company owes its suppliers at any given moment.

Trade debtors (*Accounts receivable*) The amount a company is owed by its customers at any given moment.

Trade investment A long-term investment made by one company in another for strategic, trading reasons.

Trading profit (*Operating profit, Profit before interest and tax, Earnings before interest and tax*) The profit generated by the *enterprise* of a company; i.e. profit before taking account of *interest* (either payable or receivable) and *corporation tax*.

Transaction Anything a company does which affects its financial position (and therefore its *balance sheet*).

Trend analysis Method of assessing a company by analysing the trends in its performance measures over a period of time.

Trial balance (TB) A list of all the *nominal accounts*, showing the balance in each. It is, in effect, a very detailed *balance sheet*.

Turnover (*Sales*) The total *revenues* of a company in an *accounting period*.

Value added The difference between a company's *outputs* and *inputs*.

Variable cost An *expense* which changes even with small changes in volume (e.g. raw materials costs).

Work in progress Goods due for sale but still in the course of production at the *balance sheet date*.

Working capital The amount of additional funding required by a company to operate its *fixed assets*, e.g. money to pay staff and bills while waiting for customers to pay. Working capital is equal to *capital employed* less *fixed assets*.

Working capital productivity *Sales* divided by *working capital*.

Wind up Cease trading and *liquidate* a company.

Write up/down/off Revalue an *asset* (upwards, downwards or down to zero).

Appendix

WINGATE FOODS PLC

DIRECTORS' REPORT

The directors submit their report and the audited financial statements for year five.

Review of the business and results

The principal activity of the company continues to be the production and sale of confectionery and biscuits.

Sales increased by 21.1 per cent from £8.6m in year four to £10.4m in year five. Profit before tax increased by 8.1 per cent from £583,000 in year four to £630,000 in year five.

The directors propose the payment of a final dividend of 15.4p per share for year five (year four: 13.1p).

Directors and their interests

The directors at 31 December, year five, and throughout the year ended on that date and their interests in the shares of the company were as follows:

	Fully paid Ordinary Shares	
	Year 5	Year 4
Director A	65,000	65,000
Director B	45,000	45,000
Director C	12,000	12,000
Director D	—	—
Director E	—	—

Tangible fixed assets

The changes in the tangible fixed assets are described in Note 9 to the accounts. The directors believe that the market value of the properties is at least that stated in the balance sheet.

Shareholders

At 21 March, year six, the company was not aware of any shareholders, other than directors of the company, who held 3 per cent or more of the ordinary share capital in issue.

Auditors

ABC Accountants have expressed their willingness to continue to act as the company's auditors. A resolution proposing their reappointment will be submitted at the Annual General Meeting.

By order of the Board

ANO Secretary

Secretary

31 March, year six

INDEPENDENT REPORT OF THE AUDITORS TO THE MEMBERS OF WINGATE FOODS PLC

We have audited the financial statements on pages 278 to 281, which have been prepared under the historical cost convention and the accounting policies set out on page 282.

Respective responsibilities of directors and auditors

The company's directors are responsible for the preparation of the accounts in accordance with applicable law and United Kingdom Accounting Standards.

It is our responsibility to audit the accounts in accordance with relevant legal and regulatory requirements and United Kingdom Auditing Standards.

We report to you our opinion as to whether the accounts give a true and fair view and are properly prepared in accordance with the Companies Act 1985. We also report to you if, in our opinion, the directors' report is not consistent with the accounts, if the company has not kept proper accounting records, if we have not received all the information and explanations we require for our audit, or if information specified by law regarding directors' remuneration and transactions with the company is not disclosed.

We read the directors' report and consider the implications for our report if we become aware of any apparent misstatements within it.

Basis of opinion

We conducted our audit in accordance with United Kingdom Auditing Standards issued by the Auditing Practices Board. An audit includes examination, on a test basis, of evidence relevant to the amounts and disclosures in the financial statements. It also includes an assessment of the significant estimates and judgements made by the directors in the preparation of the financial statements, and of whether the accounting policies are appropriate to the company's circumstances, consistently applied and adequately disclosed.

We planned and performed our audit so as to obtain all the information and explanations which we considered necessary in order to provide us with sufficient evidence to give reasonable assurance that the financial statements are free from material misstatement, whether caused by fraud or other irregularity or error. In forming our opinion we also evaluated the overall adequacy of the presentation of information in the financial statements.

Opinion

In our opinion, the financial statements give a true and fair view of the state of affairs of the company as at 31 December, year five, and of its results for the year then ended and have been properly prepared in accordance with the Companies Act 1985.

ABC Accountants

31 March, year six

WINGATE FOODS PLC

PROFIT AND LOSS ACCOUNT FOR YEAR FIVE

	Notes	£'000 Year 5	£'000 Year 4
Turnover	2	10,437	8,619
Cost of sales		(8,078)	(6,628)
Gross profit		2,359	1,991
Distribution expenses		(981)	(802)
Administration expenses		(449)	(362)
Operating profit	3	929	827
Interest payable	5	(299)	(244)
Profit before tax		630	583
Taxation	6	(202)	(193)
Profit after tax		428	390
Extraordinary items	7	(6)	–
Profit for the year		422	390
Dividends	8	(154)	(131)
Retained profit for the year		268	259
Earnings per share		42.2p	39.0p

There were no recognised gains or losses other than the profit for the year.

WINGATE FOODS PLC

BALANCE SHEET AT 31 DECEMBER, YEAR FIVE

	Notes	£'000 Year 5	£'000 Year 4
Fixed assets			
Tangible assets	9	5,326	4,445
Current assets			
Stock	10	1,241	953
Debtors	11	1,561	1,191
Cash		15	20
Total current assets		2,817	2,164
Current liabilities	12	2,372	1,856
Long-term liabilities	13	3,000	2,250
NET ASSETS		**2,771**	**2,503**
Shareholders' equity			
Share capital	14	50	50
Share premium		275	275
Retained profit		2,446	2,178
Total shareholders' equity		**2,771**	**2,503**

Director A

Director B

31 March, year six

WINGATE FOODS PLC

CASH FLOW STATEMENT FOR YEAR FIVE

	£'000 Year 5	£'000 Year 4
Operating activities		
Operating profit	929	827
Depreciation	495	402
Profit on sale of fixed assets	(8)	–
Increase in stock	(288)	(172)
Increase in debtors	(370)	(241)
Increase in creditors	204	75
Extraordinary items	(6)	–
Cash flow from operating activities	956	891
Returns on investments and servicing of finance		
Interest paid	(299)	(244)
Total	(299)	(244)
Taxation		
Corporation tax paid	(193)	(190)
Total taxation	(193)	(190)
Capital expenditure		
Purchase of fixed assets	(1,391)	(1,204)
Proceeds on sale of fixed assets	23	–
Total capital expenditure	(1,368)	(1,204)
Equity dividends paid		
Dividends on ordinary shares	(131)	(113)
Total equity dividends paid	(131)	(113)
Financing		
Loans obtained	750	750
Total financing	750	750
Decrease in cash	**(285)**	**(110)**

Reconciliation of net cash flow to movement in net debt

Decrease in cash	(285)	(110)
Loans obtained	(750)	(750)
Change in net debt	(1,035)	(860)
Net debt at start of year	(2,843)	(1,983)
Net debt at end of year	(3,878)	(2,843)

Analysis of changes in net debt

	At start of Year 5 £'000	Cash flows £'000	At end of Year 5 £'000
Cash	20	(5)	15
Bank overdraft	(613)	(280)	(893)
		(285)	
Bank loans	(2,250)	(750)	(3,000)
Total	(2,843)	(1,035)	(3,878)

WINGATE FOODS PLC

NOTES TO THE ACCOUNTS FOR YEAR FIVE

1 **ACCOUNTING POLICIES**

(a) **Basis of accounting**
The accounts have been prepared under the historical cost convention.

(b) **Turnover**
Turnover represents the invoiced value of goods sold net of value added tax.

(c) **Tangible fixed assets**
Depreciation is provided at rates calculated to write off the cost of each asset evenly over its expected useful life as follows:

Freehold buildings	2 per cent straight line basis
Plant and equipment	10 per cent or 20 per cent straight line basis
Motor vehicles	25 per cent straight line basis

Land is not depreciated.

(d) **Stocks**
Manufactured goods include the costs of production. Stock and work in progress are valued at the lower of cost and net realisable value. Bought in goods are valued at purchase cost on a first in first out basis.

2 **TURNOVER AND PROFIT**
Turnover is stated net of value added tax. Turnover and profit before taxation are attributable to the one principal activity.

	£'000 Year 5	£'000 Year 4
3 **OPERATING PROFIT**		
Operating profit is stated after crediting/ (charging):		
Depreciation of tangible fixed assets	(495)	(402)
Auditors' remuneration	(22)	(19)
Profit on sale of fixed assets	8	–
Hire of plant and machinery	(17)	(12)
Total	(526)	(433)

		£'000	£'000
4	**EMPLOYEES**	**Year 5**	**Year 4**

4 EMPLOYEES

The average number of employees during year was as follows:

	£'000 Year 5	£'000 Year 4
Office and management	34	28
Manufacturing	47	41
Total	81	69

Staff costs during the year amounted to:

Wages and salaries	1,211	983
Social security and pension costs	142	100
Total	1,353	1,083

Directors' remuneration

Emoluments (including pension contributions)	221	194
Emoluments of highest paid director (excluding pension contributions)	65	59

5 INTEREST PAYABLE

Overdraft and loans	299	244

6 TAXATION

The tax charge on the profit on ordinary activities for the year was as follows:

Corporation tax on the adjusted results for the year	202	193

7 EXTRAORDINARY ITEMS

Unrecovered portion of ransom payment made on kidnap of employee	6	–

	£'000	£'000
8 DIVIDENDS	**Year 5**	**Year 4**
Proposed dividend on ordinary shares	154	131

9 TANGIBLE FIXED ASSETS

	Land and Buildings £'000	Plant and Equipment £'000	Motor Vehicles £'000	Total £'000
Cost				
At start of year 5	3,401	2,503	588	6,492
Additions	570	656	165	1,391
Disposals	–	(35)	–	(35)
At end of year 5	3,971	3,124	753	7,848
Depreciation				
At start of year 5	269	1,430	348	2,047
On disposals	–	(20)	–	(20)
Charge for the year	46	345	104	495
At end of year 5	315	1,755	452	2,522
Net book value				
At start of year 5	3,132	1,073	240	4,445
At end of year 5	3,656	1,369	301	5,326

	£'000	£'000
	Year 5	**Year 4**
10 STOCKS AND WORK IN PROGRESS		
Raw materials	362	287
Work in progress	17	12
Finished goods	862	654
Total	1,241	953

	£'000	£'000
11 DEBTORS		
Trade debtors less provision for doubtful debts	1,437	1,087
Prepayments	88	76
Other debtors	36	28
Total	1,561	1,191

	£'000	£'000
	Year 5	Year 4
12 CURRENT LIABILITIES		
Trade creditors	850	701
Social security and other taxes	140	115
Accruals	113	93
Cash in advance	20	10
Sub-total	1,123	919
Bank overdraft	893	613
Taxation	202	193
Proposed dividend	154	131
Total	2,372	1,856
13 LONG-TERM LIABILITIES		
Bank loans	3,000	2,250

The loans are secured by a charge over the company's assets.

14 CALLED UP SHARE CAPITAL

Authorised

1,500,000 ordinary shares of 5p each	75	75

Issued and fully paid

1,000,000 ordinary shares of 5p each	50	50

15 FINANCIAL COMMITMENTS

At 31 December, year five, the company was committed to the future purchase of plant and equipment at a total cost of £126,300 (year four: £287,800).

Index

the bestselling guide to getting things done

SIMPLY BRILLIANT

The competitive advantage
of common sense
Fergus O'Connell

ISBN 0 273 65418 7

"Simply Brilliant is brilliantly simple – so much so that I might start coming to work to get things done." *Financial Times*

"Tears down management as a complex science, reducing it to life saving basics. This book does a good job – it may just help to simplify your working life" *Evening Standard*

"O'Connell's ideas for creating a better working environment are as simple as he claims and will provide welcome relief for anyone who is struggling to come to terms with the latest fad from the Harvard Business School…" *The Sunday Times*

Life is complicated enough. Yet many people go out of their way to create hoops to jump through, wrestling with tough problems and calling on the latest management fad to find that elusive solution to a problem. But it doesn't have to be that way. The best ideas aren't always complicated. The world is full of smart, experienced, skilled, brilliant people. However, many people – even smart ones – are lacking a set of essential skills that when pulled together can be termed 'common sense'. Shortlisted for the WHS Business Book of the Year 2002 and a runaway international bestseller, *Simply Brilliant* features a set of seven principles to make the bright better. Principles of common sense that can be adapted for attacking many of the problems that you encounter every day, be it in work or outside.

Simply Brilliant – you'll be amazed at the difference it can make.

Visit our website at
www.business-minds.com

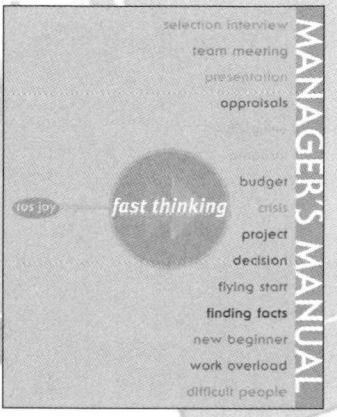

Fast Thinking
Managers Manual

Working at the speed of life

Ros Jay

0273 65298 2

It's a fast world with tight deadlines and you squeezed in between. What you need are fast solutions to help you think at the speed of life. This essential manual gives the clever tips and vital information you need to make the best of your last minute preparation. You'll look good. They'll never know.

The Fast Thinking Managers Manual – it is big and it is clever.

Topics covered:
Appraisal, Proposal, Presentation, Selection Interview, Budget, Team Meeting, Work Overload, Crisis, Finding Facts, Decision, Difficult People, Project, Discipline, and Flying Start, New Beginner

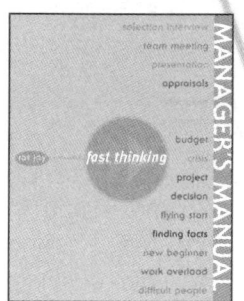